COLORADO
MOUNTAIN CLUB
PACK GUIDE

THE BEST Telluride HIKES

AF797802

ROD MARTINEZ

The Colorado Mountain Club Press
Golden, Colorado

The Best Telluride Hikes
© 2014 by The Colorado Mountain Club

All rights reserved. No part of this publication may be reproduced or transmitted in any form or by any means, electronic or mechanical, including photocopy, recording, or by any information storage and retrieval system without permission in writing from the publisher.

PUBLISHED BY
The Colorado Mountain Club Press
710 Tenth Street, Suite 200, Golden, Colorado 80401
303-996-2743 e-mail: cmcpress@cmc.org

Founded in 1912, The Colorado Mountain Club is the largest outdoor recreation, education, and conservation organization in the Rocky Mountains. Look for our books at your local bookstore or outdoor retailer or online at www.cmc.org/store.

Erika K. Arroyo: design, composition, and production
Eduard B. Avis: copy editor
Christian Green: publisher
Rod Martinez: project manager
Jeff Eisele: editor

CONTACTING THE PUBLISHER
We would appreciate it if readers would alert us to any errors or outdated information by contacting us at the address above.

DISTRIBUTED TO THE BOOK TRADE BY
The Mountaineers Books, 1001 SW Klickitat Way, Suite 201, Seattle, WA 98134, 800-553-4453, www.mountaineersbooks.org

TOPOGRAPHIC MAPS are copyright 2009 and were created using National Geographic TOPO! Outdoor Recreation software (www.natgeomaps.com; 800-962-1643).

COVER PHOTO: Lizard Head, from Cross Mountain Trail.
Photo by Rod Martinez

We gratefully acknowledge the financial support of the people of Colorado through the Scientific and Cultural Facilities District of greater Denver for our publishing activities.

WARNING: Although there has been an effort to make the trail descriptions in this book as accurate as possible, some discrepancies may exist between the text and the trails in the field. Hiking in mountainous areas—and canyons and deserts as well—is a high-risk activity. This guidebook is not a substitute for your experience and common sense. The users of this guidebook assume full responsibility for their own safety. Weather, terrain conditions, and individual abilities must be considered before undertaking any of the hikes in this guide.

First Edition

ISBN 978-1-937052-07-2

Printed in Korea

To the two great Sues in my life: my wonderful wife, Sue, of almost 45 years, who lets me escape to the beauty of Colorado that I love to hike and photograph; and my sister, Sue, who has been a great friend and buddy for more years than she wants me to say. This book also highlights many of the trails my sons, John and Chris, have hiked with me. Most important, it is for my granddaughters, Brittany, Nichole, and Samantha, and other young people who I hope will enjoy the outdoors and photographing it so others can share in the beauty that surrounds us as much as I have. Finally, to my great hiking friend Jerry Shallman, who now resides in Minnesota and is sorely missed.

—Rod Martinez
September 2013

Early fall in the Sneffels Range, as seen from the Blaine Basin Trail.
PHOTO BY ROD MARTINEZ

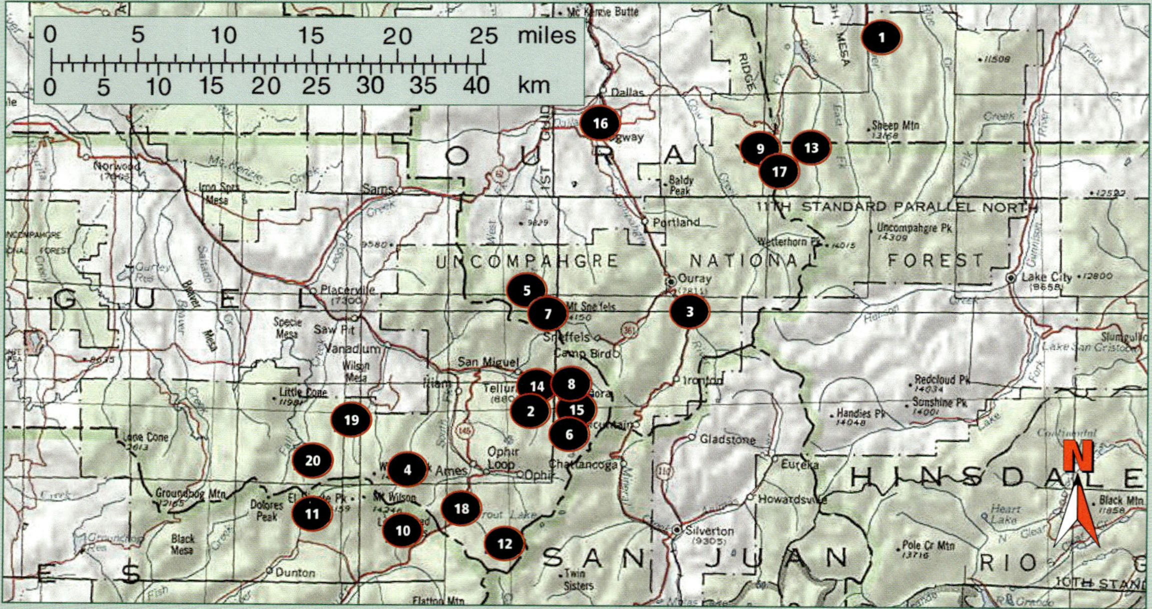
0 5 10 15 20 25 miles
0 5 10 15 20 25 30 35 40 km
N
UNCOMPAHGRE NATIONAL FOREST
11TH STANDARD PARALLEL NORTH
OURAY
SAN JUAN
HINSDALE
Dallas
Ridgway
Portland
Ouray
Lake City
Norwood
Placerville
Sawpit
Vanadium
San Miguel
Ilium
Ophir
Ophir Loop
Ames
Chattanooga
Silverton
Gladstone
Eureka
Howardsville
Ironton
Camp Bird
Sneffels
Dunton
Sams
Mt Sneffels
Wetterhorn Pk
Uncompahgre Pk
Sheep Mtn
Baldy Peak
Redcloud Pk
Sunshine Pk
Handies Pk
Pole Cr Mtn
Black Mtn
Dolores Peak
Groundhog Mtn
Lone Cone
Little Cone
Black Mesa
Specie Mesa
Wilson Mesa
Iron Spgs Mesa
Twin Sisters
Flattop Mtn
Mt Wilson
Heart Lake
1 2 3 4 5 6 7 8 9 10 11 12 13 14 15 16 17 18 19 20

CONTENTS

THE HIKES

Up close with some waterfalls on the east fork of Dallas Creek, as it leaves Lower Blue Lake next to Mount Sneffels. PHOTO BY ROD MARTINEZ

180

FOREWORD

The 20 hiking trails in this pack guide range from the alpine trails of the Cimarron Range of the San Juan Mountains to the more mountainous terrain of the San Miguels. In between these two areas, you can explore the Sneffels Range of the San Juans. Before you tackle the hikes ranked moderate or difficult, I recommend you become acclimated to the altitude.

RATINGS

What distinguishes the difficulty rating of the hikes? Each hiker will see differences in what is termed easy, moderate, and difficult. Among elements in establishing the ratings are:

Elevation gain. A 1,700-foot gain in elevation for a round-trip hike of 3 to 4 miles may be as difficult or as strenuous as one gaining 3,000 feet in a 6- to 8-mile round trip.

Round-trip distance. Normally, an 8- to 10-mile hike is more difficult or strenuous than one of 4 to 6 miles.

Trail characteristics. Is the trail well marked, or do you need to search for continuation of the trail? Are boulder hopping or scree slopes involved? Are there creek/stream crossings, and are they easy or is wading involved? As the difficult elements add up or increase in severity, so will the difficulty rating.

WEATHER

Be aware of and prepared for changes in the weather. If it looks as if it will rain, consider doing the hike another day. An early start will decrease the odds of encountering afternoon thunderstorms. If the weather begins to deteriorate while you are hiking, be cautious and consider turning around.

Once while ascending the Electric Pass Trail, near Aspen, I noticed clouds were beginning to build. After reaching the pass, the clouds were really gathering and the wind began to blow. Instead of relaxing, I quickly turned around and headed back. I talked with other hikers on their way up who seemed unconcerned about the weather, and they did not appear to be carrying any rain gear. About 10:30 AM, I passed more hikers still going up as it began to rain. Shortly thereafter, I cleared the first ridge before the clouds opened up and it began to rain rather hard. I put on my rain jacket and kept going down. In another 0.5 mile, the rain became intense and it started to hail. I finally descended from the last ridge and entered the trees before the storm intensified with flashes of lightning. Because I had the proper equipment and was cautious, I returned safely. Situations such as this are not unusual in the mountains. Don't take chances when the weather is changing.

ROUND-TRIP TIME

The time it takes to complete a hike depends on the physical ability of the hiker and the purpose of the hike. The hikes described in this pack guide might be among the first hikes for some readers, and consequently, it might take them longer to get acclimated to the altitude and tune up muscles little used before. Others might be acclimated and in great shape. The time it takes them to complete these hikes might be considerably shorter.

I happen to be a slow hiker, because I pause frequently to catch my breath and enjoy the scenery. I also stop and take a lot of photographs. I am not a point-and-shoot photographer. I work at getting the best possible photo (see photography tips on page 18 of this pack guide), so it might take more time to capture the image I am seeking.

The times listed in this pack guide are based on average hikers who want to enjoy their hike. For those who hike for great outdoor exercise, the times probably will be shorter. I recommend you start early to avoid afternoon storms, and begin your return trip in time to make it to the trailhead before it gets dark.

SAFETY

The Ten Essentials Systems, on pages 15-17 of this pack guide, are the Colorado Mountain Club's "systems" to promote safety awareness and give you a list of safety items to carry with you at all times when hiking. Please take the time to read, study, and absorb all the Ten Essentials.

Here are some additional safety measures to consider and make habits:

- Tell someone where you plan to go and when you plan to return. Be specific and stay on the trail. Tell that person to contact authorities in the area you are hiking if he or she does not hear from you by an appointed time.
- Sign in at the trail register. Sign out when you return.
- Consider carrying an emergency locater device. In life-threatening circumstances, it can notify emergency personnel where you are and that you need their help. Keep it readily accessible so you can reach it when necessary. When not hiking, keep it in your vehicle—just in case. There are several available with various features at outdoor equipment retailers.
- Consider purchasing a CORSAR (Colorado Outdoor Recreation Search and Rescue) card. Colorado has a Search and Rescue Fund to help local agencies cover the costs of search-and-rescue operations. Money for the fund is provided by a surcharge on hunting and fishing licenses and vessel, snowmobile, and off-highway vehicle registrations. People who don't have one of those licenses, registrations, or a CORSAR card could be billed for some expenses related to a search and rescue, which can be extensive. A CORSAR card costs $3 annually or $12 for a five-year card. You can purchase a CORSAR card from outdoor, recreation, and sporting goods retailers and organizations throughout the state. It also can

be purchased online; simply search for CORSAR for a link to the state website.

LEAVE NO TRACE

We owe it to present and future generations to care for the wild places. If you pack it in, pack it out—leave only footprints:

- Plan ahead and prepare for the cleanest possible adventure.
- Stay on the trail and don't shortcut on switchbacks; camp on durable surfaces, such as rock or sand. Above timberline, hike on rocks and avoid damaging the tundra. When more than one person is off trail, spread out so you don't start destructive new "social" trails.
- Dispose of all waste properly, including that deposited by your dog. "Pack it in, pack it out."
- Leave what you find—look at it, take a photo, leave it for the next person.
- Minimize campfire impacts—think small and keep the fuel within the fire circle. Unless it is a permanent fire pit, destroy all traces of your fire before leaving your campsite. Forest fires have started from small camp fires or their smoldering embers; be extremely cautious in this regard. The best practice is to soak down your fire site.
- Respect wildlife—don't feed them anything and don't intrude on their feeding and breeding areas. Moose deserve your complete respect; they are considered by experts to be the most dangerous creatures in the Colorado woods.
- Be considerate of animals and other humans in the woods—don't play your radio or make other unnecessary noise. Part of the lure of the woods is the healing sound of wind through the trees, or the murmur of a stream.

ACKNOWLEDGMENTS

This pack guide required the efforts of a number of talented people to hike the trails, write the narratives, and take photographs: Diana Donnelly, Jeff Eisele, Christian Green, Sandy Hoagland, Rod Martinez, Laura Scull, Laszlo Szuecs, Bernadette Tuthill, and Chip Tuthill.

Without these folks persevering and volunteering their valuable time, this pack guide would not have been accomplished at this time.

Without the support and encouragement of all members of the Western Slope and San Juan groups of the Colorado Mountain Club, this pack guide would have been a task rather than a pleasure.

Thanks to Christian Green, publisher at Colorado Mountain Club Press, for his expert guidance and terrific selection of the cover photo.

A big thanks must go to Jeff Eisele. His help to a novice author and rework of content for this book relieved the challenge and self-imposed frustration.

Happy trails to all!

—Rod Martinez

Colorado's state flower—the blue columbine.

PHOTO BY ROD MARTINEZ

Introduction

Telluride is truly an area for all seasons. Telluride Ski Resort is well known for plentiful snow and distinct ski runs. In the spring, the waterfalls near Telluride (Cornet Creek, Ingram, Bear Creek, and Bridal Veil) are fabulous to enjoy and photograph as they cascade down the sides of the surrounding mountains. In early summer, the wildflowers begin to explode with color and abundance. During fall, the changing aspens spread gold on every mountainside traversed by each trail in this pack guide. You might want to come back and rehike a number of these trails when the leaves are changing, the temperature is cooler and crisper, and a dusting of snow might be evident on the higher peaks.

But this pack guide includes more than Telluride. You can enjoy trails south of town near Rico and east to Owl Creek Pass and Silver Jack Reservoir with stops in between in the Ouray and Ridgway areas. All of these places are equally beautiful and adventurous.

The beauty and ruggedness of the mountains is what makes this area a premier place to hike. The 99,000 acres of the Uncompahgre Wilderness contain Uncompahgre Peak (14,309 feet), Wetterhorn Peak (14,015), and many others above 13,000 feet. Among them are Sheep Mountain, Silver Mountain, Matter-

Caveat—on maps and map scales

In producing this pack guide, we have endeavored to provide the most accurate information possible. This striving for accuracy includes the map segments which follow each trail description. Many of the trails indicated by the red lines, however, include contours, ups and downs, and switchbacks that cannot be depicted on a small map. Thus, with some maps, you may find what looks like a variance between the stated length of the trail and the length of the trail when compared to the scale indicator.

For every trail described in this guide, we list relevant, larger-scale maps of the area you will be hiking in—such as Trails Illustrated and USGS maps. It is always a good practice to secure these larger maps, study them, and understand where the smaller map from the guide fits within the larger map. The best practice is to carry both maps on your hike.

Busy bees gathering pollen to help generate more wildflowers.
PHOTO BY ROD MARTINEZ

horn, Coxcomb, Precipice, Redcliff, and the incomparable Chimney Rock (11,781) and Courthouse Mountain (12,152).

The 16,500 acres of the Mount Sneffels Wilderness is home to Mount Sneffels (14,150), which is dubbed the "Queen of the San Juans." This wilderness area, too, has many peaks rising above 13,000 feet.

The 41,193 acres of the Lizard Head Wilderness encompass part of the San Miguel Mountains, including El Diente (14,159), Wilson Peak (14,017), and Mount Wilson (14,246), as well as the hard-to-climb Gladstone Peak (13,913) and the rarely climbed Lizard Head (13,113).

Gold and silver ore brought people in the late 19th century to build and work the many mines that dot these mountains from Ouray to Telluride. You will pass many inactive mines as you hike the trails in this pack guide. Take caution, as there are rusty nails that could puncture boots, deep mine shafts, and old buildings that could tumble at your touch. With the mining came towns that were home to the miners long before they became tourist meccas and homes to "modern-day mountaineers" who love being close to the mountains and wilderness all year long. Please respect their private property and stay on the maintained roads and trails.

The towns of Telluride, Ouray, and Ridgway offer many amenities and entertainment venues you would expect in most towns. The difference here is the cozy atmosphere. Telluride is a National Historic District with numerous Victorian homes, ornate churches, an old cemetery, and an old school building that make for great viewing as you walk the San Miguel River Trail. Ouray is a small, intimate community nestled in some of the most rugged and towering peaks of the Rockies. It sits at the head of a valley at almost 8,000 feet elevation and is surrounded on three sides by 13,000-foot, snowcapped peaks.

Hundreds of miles of historic four-wheel-drive roads (high-clearance vehicles required on most of these) lead to world-renowned wildflower meccas such as Yankee Boy Basin and American Basin. Enjoy the stunning views of the mountains as you lay back and relax in one of the sulfur-free hot springs that dot the area.

In the wintertime, Ouray hosts world-class ice climbing at the Ouray Ice Park. It also is the gateway to the Uncompahgre Gorge and Red Mountain Pass south of town, a beautiful area in fall and winter.

Ridgway is nestled in the picturesque Uncompahgre River Valley surrounded by the majestic snowcapped peaks of the Cimarron and San Juan mountain ranges. Ridgway is the northern entrance of the San Juan Scenic and Historic Byway, one of America's most spectacular highways. The town also is home to Dennis Weaver Memorial Park, dedicated to the well-known actor and, more recently, respected environmentalist.

From the Cimarrons on the east, through the Sneffels Range to the San Miguels in the southwest, this pack guide offers a wide variety of trails that can be hiked from spring through fall. Enjoy!

The Ten Essentials Systems

The Colorado Mountain Club (CMC), through CMC Press, is the publisher of this pack guide. For 100 years, CMC has fostered safety awareness and safe practices in the wilderness, and has distilled the essential safety items down to a list known as "The Ten Essentials." We present it here in a "systems" approach. Carrying the items from this list that are appropriate for the location, mileage, and elevation of your hike will help you be fully prepared for every trip and able to survive the unexpected emergency. We encourage all hikers to study, adopt, and teach The Ten Essentials Systems as part of their own outdoors regimen.

1. **Hydration.** Carry at least 2 liters or quarts of water on any hike. For arid country or desert hiking, carry more. Keep an extra water container in your vehicle and hydrate both before and after your hike. Don't wait until you are thirsty—stay hydrated.
2. **Nutrition.** Eat a good breakfast before your hike; pack a full and healthy lunch, including fruits, vegetables, and carbohydrates. Carry healthy snacks such as trail mix and nutrition bars.
3. **Sun protection.** Start with sunscreen with an SFP rating of at least 45 and reapply it as you hike. Wear sunglasses and a wide-brimmed hat, and use lip balm. These protections are important anywhere in Colorado, especially at high elevations and in desert areas.
4. **Insulation.** Be aware that weather in Colorado can go through extreme changes in a very short time. Think warm and think dry—even in arid areas. Dress with wool or synthetic inner and outer layers. Cotton retains moisture and does not insulate well; it should not be part of your hiking gear. Carry a warm hat, gloves, and

13,752-foot San Miguel Peak from Lake Hope Trail.

PHOTO BY ROD MARTINEZ

extra socks. Always include a rain/wind parka and rain pants—on you or in your pack. Extra clothing weighs little and is a great safety component.

5. **Navigation.** You should attain at least minimal proficiency with a map and compass. A GPS unit can add to your ability, but it's not a substitute for the two basics. Before a hike, study your route, and the surrounding country, on a good map of the area. Refer to the map as needed on the trail.
6. **Illumination.** Include a headlamp or flashlight in your gear, preferably both. With a headlamp, your hands are kept free. Avoid hiking in the dark if at all possible.

7. **First Aid.** Buy or assemble an adequate first-aid kit. Some items to include:
    - Ace bandages; a bandana, which can double as a sling.
    - Duct tape—good for a bandage, blister protection, or rips in your clothes.
    - A small bottle of alcohol or hydrogen peroxide for cleaning a wound.
    - Latex gloves.
    - Specific medications for you and your companions.
    - Toilet paper and Ziploc bags for carrying it out.

Note: this is not a comprehensive list—tailor it and add items for your own perceived needs and intended activities.

8. **Fire.** The best practice is to avoid open fires except in emergency situations. For when you may need to build a fire, carry waterproof matches in a watertight container, a lighter, or a commercial fire starter such as a fire ribbon. Keep these items dry and ensure that all of them will work in cold or wet weather. If needed, tree sap or dry pine needles can help start a fire.
9. **Repair kit and emergency tools.** A pocketknife or multitool and duct tape or electrician's tape are good for various repairs. For emergencies, carry a whistle and signal mirror.
10. **Emergency shelter.** Carry a space blanket and nylon cord or a bivouac sack. Large plastic leaf bags are handy for temporary rain gear, pack covers, or survival shelters. On your way out, use this for trash left by careless hikers.

Photography Tips

We see many beautiful subjects in the outdoors that we would like to remember. Here are a few tips to help you take great photographs and enjoy, time and again, the places where you've been:

- Don't forget to take your camera with you. As you hike, keep it within easy reach.
- Carry extra memory cards so you can take enough photographs to properly record your hike and what you saw.
- Charge your batteries before leaving and take extras if you will be out more than one day.
- Before leaving home, set your camera's resolution to the highest setting possible. Check your manual to see how to do this. Another name for resolution is image quality. You want to use every pixel that you paid for when you bought your camera. A higher setting will give you the ability to capture the light and dark tones as well as all the colors your eyes can see.
- Be prepared. Most hikes start early in the morning, so have your camera out and be prepared to capture the early-morning light on the mountains or animals moving around.
- Hold your camera steady. The closer the camera is to your face, the steadier it will be. Your photo should not have that unsteady, out-of-focus look.
- Place your whole subject in the frame, and fill the frame with your subject. If you are taking photos of the mountains, be sure to include the tops. Zoom in to crop out those items that do not add to the photo. I recommend vertical photos as opposed to horizontal ones when you

A beautiful stand of tall aspens at the base of Sheep Mountain near Silver Jack Reservoir. PHOTO BY ROD MARTINEZ

are taking photos of trees, flowers, people, and other vertical objects. The vertical format allows you to increase the size of your subject as you zoom in.

- The best way to learn is from your mistakes. Take lots of photos, trying different angles and settings. Try photographing the same images twice, once with a horizontal orientation and once vertical. Remember, a memory card can be reused, and those pixels are free.
- If all else fails, read the manual.

WILDLIFE VIEWING TIPS

Fade into the woodwork (or woods): Wear natural colors and unscented lotions, if any. Be as quiet as possible—walk softly, move slowly.

A fresh blanket of snow covers Mount Sneffels.

PHOTO BY ROD MARTINEZ

Keep to the sidelines: Watch animals from a distance they consider safe. Use binoculars or a telephoto lens to get a closer view. Stay away from nests.

Use your senses

- **Eyes:** Look up, down, and all around for animal or bird signs such as scat, nests, or tracks. Learn to distinguish these wildlife signatures.
- **Ears:** Listen for animal sounds or movement.
- **Nose:** Be alert to musky scents or strange odors.

Think like an animal: When will an animal eat, nap, drink, bathe?

An old railroad trestle crosses over Lake Fork Creek.

PHOTO BY ROD MARTINEZ

Optimize your watching: The ultimate wildlife-watching experience is of behaviors—viewing animals without interrupting their normal activities. As a rule, dusk and dawn are the best times for this rewarding experience.

—*Rod Martinez*

A waterfall along the way to Lower Blue Lake.

PHOTO BY ROD MARTINEZ

1. Alpine Trail

BY ROD MARTINEZ

MAPS	Trails Illustrated, Telluride/Silverton/Ouray/Lake City, Number 141; USGS, Courthouse Mountain 7.5 minute; Latitude 40, Southwest Colorado Trails
ELEVATION GAIN	1,720 feet
RATING	Moderate
ROUND-TRIP DISTANCE	9–10 miles
ROUND-TRIP TIME	5–6 hours
NEAREST LANDMARK	Silver Jack Reservoir

COMMENT: The Alpine Trail will take you to the High Mesa Trailhead at the base of Sheep Mountain, where you will get a superb bird's-eye view of parts of the Uncompahgre Wilderness, Cimarron Ridge, and Silver Jack Reservoir. This area is dominated by a vast array of 13,000-foot mountains, dominant rock spires, canyons carved by the three arms of the Cimarron River, the reservoir, and countless groves of aspens that turn gold in the fall. The reservoir is large and scenic, providing a wide range of recreational activities, including great fishing, motorless boating, and hiking trails in all directions. If you want to take more time and savor the beauty of the area, Uncompahgre National Forest has three campgrounds: Big Cimarron, Beaver Lake, and Silver Jack.

GETTING THERE: Measure from the traffic light in Ridgway (intersection of U.S. 550 and Colorado 62). Travel 1.8 miles north on U.S. 550 and turn right (east) on County Road 10. At 2.7 miles, bear left toward Owl Creek Pass and Silver Jack Reservoir, staying on CR 10. At 4.5 miles, continue straight on CR 10. At 6 miles, bear right on CR 8. Courthouse Mountain and Chimney Rock now come into view to the southeast. Go left at 7.5 miles, staying on CR 8. The Uncompahgre National

Fall colors on the Alpine Trail. PHOTO BY ROD MARTINEZ

Forest boundary is at mile 10, where the road becomes Forest Road 858. Bear left again at 11 miles, and continue on FR 858 to Owl Creek Pass at 17 miles. At 17.3 miles, continue left on FR 858, which will take you to Silver Jack Reservoir and the Alpine Trail. After 24 miles, FR 858 intersects with FR 863. Stay left on FR 863, which will take you to the East Fork of the Cimarron River and the trailhead, 1.7 miles north of the intersection of the two forest roads. A small parking area is across the road from the signed trailhead.

THE ROUTE: There is a large open meadow at the trailhead. The trail skirts around a beautiful aspen grove and then enters the grove as you begin the ascent. The elevation gain in the beginning is minimal but starts to climb rapidly along rock spires as you switchback to the top.

The view of Silver Jack Reservoir and Cimarron Ridge across the valley expands as you ascend. It includes the 13,000-foot peaks of Precipice, Redcliff, and Coxcomb, as well as the distinct Chimney Rock and Courthouse Mountain to the southwest. Down valley are distant views of Matterhorn Peak and, on a clear day, the Fourteeners Uncompahgre and Wetterhorn peaks. The closest and most dominant peak to the southeast is 13,168-foot Sheep Mountain.

Pinnacles tower over the trail on the mesa. PHOTO BY ROD MARTINEZ

The trail levels out as you reach the top, where it eventually crosses some old roads and then intersects with Trail #229, which, if followed north, takes you down to the Little Cimarron Trailhead or, if followed south, takes you to a spur trail leading to the top of Sheep Mountain. It is recommended that you turn around here or a little earlier at the intersection of Trail #123, which also leads to Sheep Mountain.

In late spring and early summer the top can be very wet and boggy. There also are a number of downed trees to skirt around as you hike on top of the mesa. This is an excellent place to take a break and then turn around and retrace your steps to the Alpine Trailhead.

Distinctive Chimney Rock comes into view as you ascend the Alpine Trail. PHOTO BY ROD MARTINEZ

This trail is open to motorized trail bikes, which I have encountered during some summer weekends. It is best hiked during early fall, when the aspens are in their colorful glory.

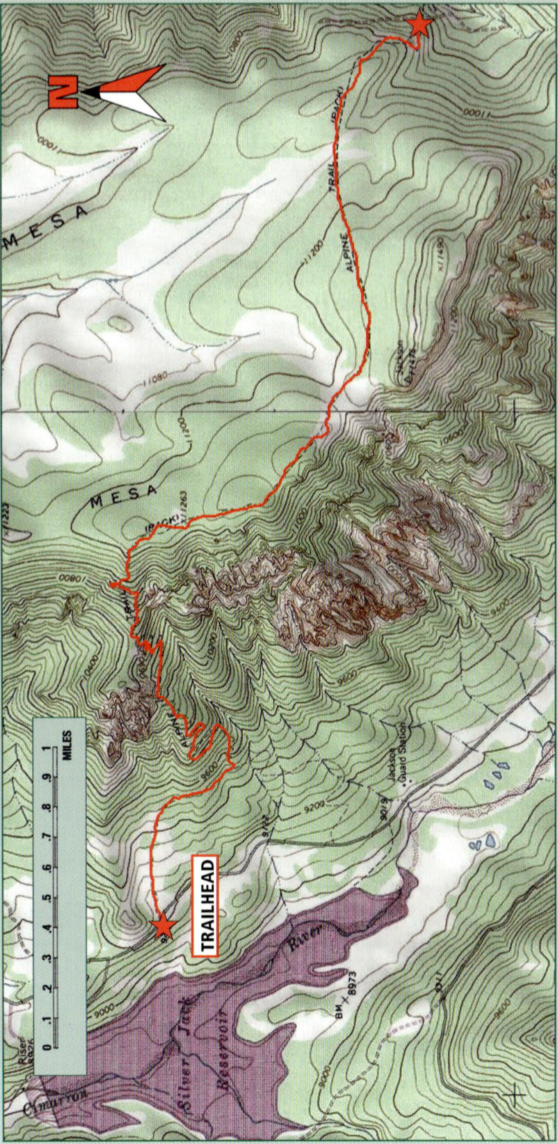
N
MESA
MESA
ALPINE TRAIL (PACK)
TRAILHEAD
MILES
0 .1 .2 .3 .4 .5 .6 .7 .8 .9 1
Jackson Guard Station
Silver Jack Reservoir
River
Cimarron
BM 8973

2. Bear Creek Falls Trail

BY BERNADETTE AND CHIP TUTHILL

MAPS	Trails Illustrated, Telluride/Silverton/Ouray/Lake City, Number 141; USGS, Telluride 7.5 minute; Latitude 40, Telluride/Silverton/Ouray Trails
ELEVATION GAIN	1,050 feet
RATING	Easy
ROUND-TRIP DISTANCE	4.0 miles
ROUND-TRIP TIME	3–4 hours
NEAREST LANDMARK	Telluride

COMMENT: This trail is a relatively easy uphill hike that follows an old mining road up a canyon through the Bear Creek Preserve. The San Miguel Conservation Foundation and the town of Telluride acquired the original 320 acres of the Bear Creek Preserve in 1995 as public open space. The preserve since has expanded and now encompasses almost 400 acres of this spectacular mountain canyon.

There are remnants of the foundations of the Bear Creek Mill that belonged to the San Miguel Consolidated Gold Mining Co. and once was owned by electric power pioneer L.L. Nunn. The trail is open year-round, but accessibility in winter depends on snow conditions. Dogs are permitted.

GETTING THERE: The trail starts at the south end of Pine Street in Telluride, four blocks south of Colorado Avenue (the main east-west street that becomes Colorado 145 west of town). Paid parking is limited. A second option is to continue east on Colorado Avenue to Telluride Town Park, where there is plenty of parking and restrooms. From the park, follow the river trail to the left of the duck pond. Cross

The first view of the falls on the Bear Creek Falls Trail.

PHOTO BY CHIP TUTHILL

over a bridge and go left, along the river, to Pine Street. The trailhead is on the left in 0.25 mile.

THE ROUTE: Pass an iron gate at the trailhead where a large wooden sign invites you to share, respect, and protect the Bear Creek Preserve. The trail is an easy-to-follow dirt road that starts to climb immediately. If you are new to hiking at altitude, don't despair—there are many places along the way where the trail levels off for a breather.

Soon you will look down on a pond and beaver dam. Ahead is a kiosk with a map and points of interest about the trail. As you continue, listen for the rushing water of the creek below. Many side trails take you to the edge of the creek. You might find remnants of a flume dating to the 1890s. Take care, because the side trails might be steep or slippery. Be respectful and stay off areas that are marked for revegetation. Watch for a side trail on your left going through a small meadow. It leads to a natural flume where the water is channeled through a narrow gorge.

As you continue up the trail, there are spectacular mountain views and a waterfall to your left. You also will be treated to spectacular views of Ballard Mountain and La Junta Peak. About .75 mile from the kiosk, you'll come to

Looking down canyon at climbing boulders and a feature called The Big Rock.

PHOTO BY BERNADETTE TUTHILL

a "Garden of Cairns" (stone markers that are used to mark trails or historical or memorial sites, or are built for decorative or artistic expression). The garden of 2012 is the largest that locals have ever seen. Add your own "garden" contribution. The paths through the garden offer lovely picnic spots and views of the creek.

Continuing up the trail, watch for the remains of the Bear Creek Mill on the right. Bear right at a fork. Climb a short distance farther, and the falls come into view for the first time. Pass the Wasatch Trail on your right. When a very large rock comes into view, take a single-track trail on the right for about 0.25 mile to reach the falls.

A fine view of the falls is obtained by scrambling up a boulder before reaching the falls. Find a spot to sit and enjoy the falls and the scenery before heading back.

To return, retrace your steps, watching the scenic canyon views unfold below you along the way.

A close-up look at Bear Creek Falls. PHOTO BY BERNADETTE TUTHILL

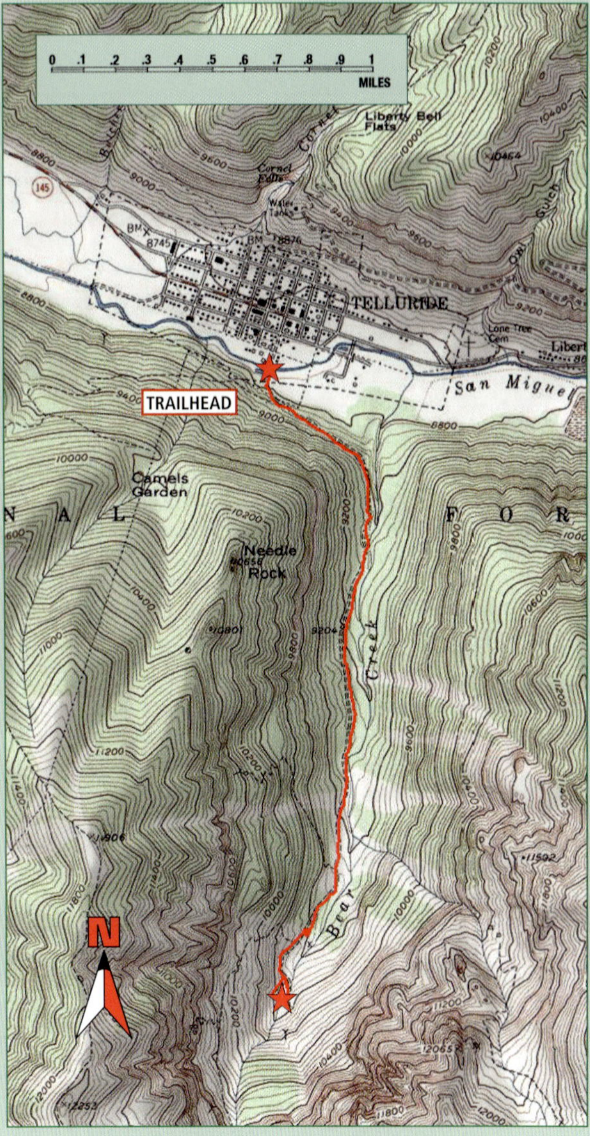
0 .1 .2 .3 .4 .5 .6 .7 .8 .9 1
MILES
TRAILHEAD
TELLURIDE
Liberty Bell Flats
Cornet Falls
Camels Garden
Needle Rock
Bear Creek
San Miguel
Lone Tree Cem
N

3. Bear Creek National Recreation Trail

BY CHRISTIAN GREEN

MAPS	Trails Illustrated, Telluride/ Silverton/Ouray/Lake City, Number 141; USGS, Ouray 7.5 minute; Latitude 40, Telluride/ Silverton/Ouray Trails
ELEVATION GAIN	2,640 feet
RATING	Moderate
ROUND-TRIP DISTANCE	8.4 miles
ROUND-TRIP TIME	6–7 hours
NEAREST LANDMARK	Ouray

COMMENT: Bear Creek Trail is not the most challenging hike, but if you are acrophobic or plan to bring your adventurous children or dogs with you, you should consider another excursion. A good portion of the trail is bounded on one side by a steep drop-off of several hundred feet with little between you and Bear Creek below. In addition, the first part of the trail is composed of crushed slate and quartzite, which could become slippery during wet weather.

That said, there's a reason Bear Creek Trail is one of only 39 trails in Colorado to be designated a National Recreation Trail. Not only do you experience breathtaking views, but you also are transported back in time. Miners detonated dynamite to construct this trail in the 1870s, because it was too rugged to build a trail along the creek bottom below, where ample gold and silver could be found. Today, the trail passes the abandoned Grizzly Bear mining camp and ends near Yellow Jacket mining camp, where visitors can peer into an old cabin to see cots the miners slept on.

A long stretch of the trail is bounded on one side by a steep drop-off.
PHOTO BY CHRISTIAN GREEN

GETTING THERE: From Ouray, drive 2.3 miles south on U.S. 550 until you reach a small tunnel. Once you pass through the tunnel, abundant parking is available on the right, next to the trailhead, and also on the left. From Telluride, head west on Colorado 145 (stay straight, rather than turning left toward Rico) for a little more than 15 miles. Turn right on Colorado 62 and drive just more than 23 miles to the town of Ridgway, where you will make a right on U.S. 550 south. Drive approximately 10 miles to Ouray and follow the directions above.

THE ROUTE: At the trailhead, take a moment to enjoy the view of Ouray a couple of miles to the north, and then cross above the tunnel. On the other side of U.S. 550, the trail gains 1,000 feet of elevation in the first 1.25 miles. There are several switch-

The remnants of Grizzly Bear mining camp.
PHOTO BY CHRISTIAN GREEN

backs in this section of the trail, which, again, can be slippery because the trail is covered in loose fragments of slate and quartzite. Although the trail levels off after traversing the switchbacks, it becomes precarious at this point, especially for those who are afraid of heights. For the next mile, the trail is bordered on the right by a very steep cliff, which drops down to Bear Creek below. Stay on the left side of the trail if you have any concerns. It's along this stretch of trail where the views really begin to open up.

At the 2.4-mile mark, you will come across the first of two mining camps along the trail—Grizzly Bear. The remnants of the camp, which was active from 1875 to around 1900, are still littered around the trail. This is a good place to grab a quick snack and take a break.

From there to Yellow Jacket mining camp, 1.8 miles away, the trail alternates between open stretches and stands of aspens and conifers as Bear Creek rises closer to the trail on the right. Around 0.3 mile past Grizzly Bear mining camp, you will cross over a small tributary of Bear Creek and enter a beautiful meadow. To your left is a picturesque hillside, framed by striking aspens.

As you gradually ascend to Yellow Jacket mining camp, Mount Sneffels (14,150 feet) rises majestically behind you. Once you reach the camp, take some time to enjoy the panoramic view of the Sneffels Range, which includes the Centennials Teakettle Mountain (13,819) and Dallas Peak (13,809), and explore the miners' quarters.

Make sure you are well rested before heading back the way you came to ensure your legs aren't wobbly when you traverse the ledge section of the trail.

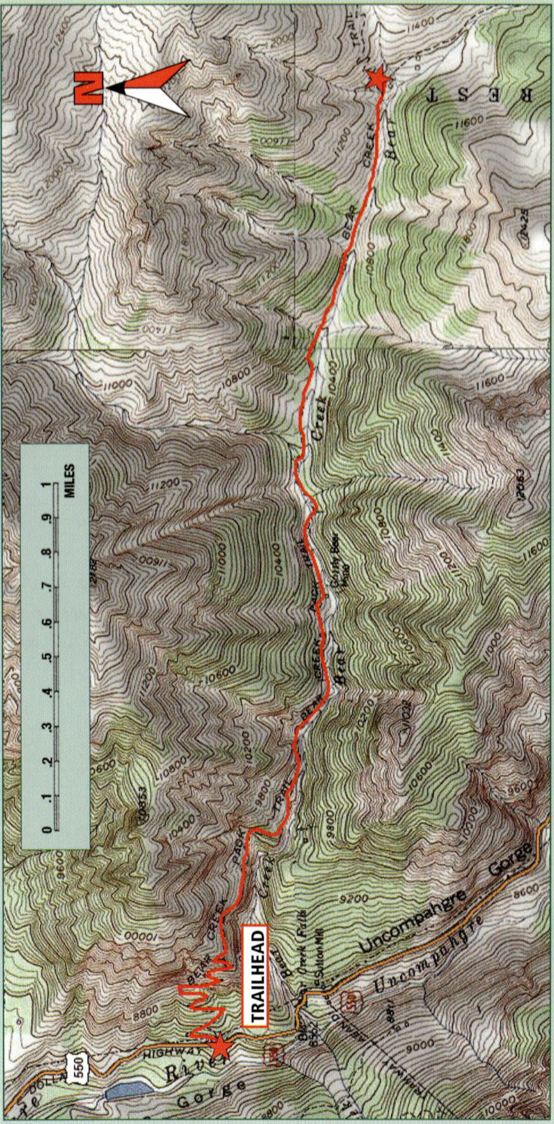

N
0 .1 .2 .3 .4 .5 .6 .7 .8 .9 1
MILES
TRAILHEAD
BEAR CREEK PACK TRAIL
Uncompahgre Gorge
HIGHWAY
550

4. Bilk Creek Basin Trail

BY ROD MARTINEZ

MAPS	Trails Illustrated, Telluride/ Silverton/Ouray/Lake City, Number 141; USGS, Gray Head and Mt. Wilson 7.5 minute; Latitude 40, Telluride/Silverton/ Ouray Trails
ELEVATION GAIN	1,600 feet
RATING	Difficult
ROUND-TRIP DISTANCE	8–9 miles
ROUND-TRIP TIME	8–10 hours
NEAREST LANDMARK	Telluride

COMMENT: This hike will take you to a beautiful basin situated at the base of several high peaks in the Wilson Group of the San Miguel Mountains—13,913-foot Gladstone Peak, Wilson Peak (14,017), Lizard Head (13,113), and Cross Mountain (12,703). From the trailhead to the basin you will hike along the side of the base of Sunshine Mountain (12,930). This mountain has a reputation as being tough to climb, and from this side, one can understand why.

The trail also will take you to the side or base of numerous waterfalls, including the Upper Bilk Creek Falls, which are more than 100 feet in length. All have their own beauty as they race and plunge down the mountainsides.

There is a difficult maneuver where the trail crosses Bilk Creek. One option is to cross a rather large log over the creek by the old, abandoned Morningstar Mine. Another is upstream, where you can work your way through and over a logjam. Either route can be tricky, especially if the water is high in late spring and early summer.

Before you cross the creek, you will encounter a large rock pile that also should be tackled cautiously. Note where you

Hikers get their first panoramic view of Mount Wilson (left center) and Gladstone Peak (right center) towering over the trail to Bilk Creek Basin.
PHOTO BY ROD MARTINEZ

are entering and leaving the rock pile so you can find the trail on your way back. Stay low on the rocks and step carefully, because the rocks may slip. Sturdy hiking boots help with secure footing.

Reaching the lower basin is unequaled in beauty and solitude.

GETTING THERE: From the "Society Turn" roundabout west of Telluride on Colorado 145, go west on 145 toward Placerville for 2.5 miles and turn left onto the Ilium/South Fork Road (County Road 63L). Go 2.1 miles up the road and turn right onto County Road 63J (Forest Road 623), more commonly known as Sunshine Mesa Road. You will pass a gravel pit and a church camp and then turn right just before reaching a bridge at the next intersection. Continue uphill for another 5.6 miles to the Sunshine Mesa Trailhead. The road is narrow, steep, and rocky at times but passable by all vehicles.

THE ROUTE: FR 623 continues on the other side of the gate at the trailhead. The old road is level as it heads up the valley to Bilk Basin. The Forest Service calls it the Morningstar Mine Trail (#409). After 1.0 mile, you will see a sign and a trail

Lizard Head peeks over the top of the ridge in Bilk Creek Basin.

PHOTO BY ROD MARTINEZ

that goes right to Wilson Mesa (#421). Stay left until you begin to see the old Morningstar Mine across Bilk Creek on your right. As you begin to work your way through the boulder pile, look for the log and/or logjam crossing of Bilk Creek. Once across the creek, you will merge with the Lizard Head Trail (#505).

After the old mine, the trail begins to switchback and climb steeply up the mountainside. You will hear and begin to see the marvelous waterfalls. The lower falls are accessible if you are cautious, as you make your way off trail to the creek bed. The wildflowers are abundant, especially columbines, as you hike between the lower and upper falls. The upper falls are more dramatic, because they plunge more than 100 feet to the lower falls.

Eventually, the trail levels off as you approach the lower basin of Bilk Creek. Take time to enjoy the creek as it meanders through the lush meadows at the base of the aforementioned high peaks. Retrace your steps to the trailhead.

The upper falls on the hike to Bilk Creek Basin plunge 100 feet.

PHOTO BY ROD MARTINEZ

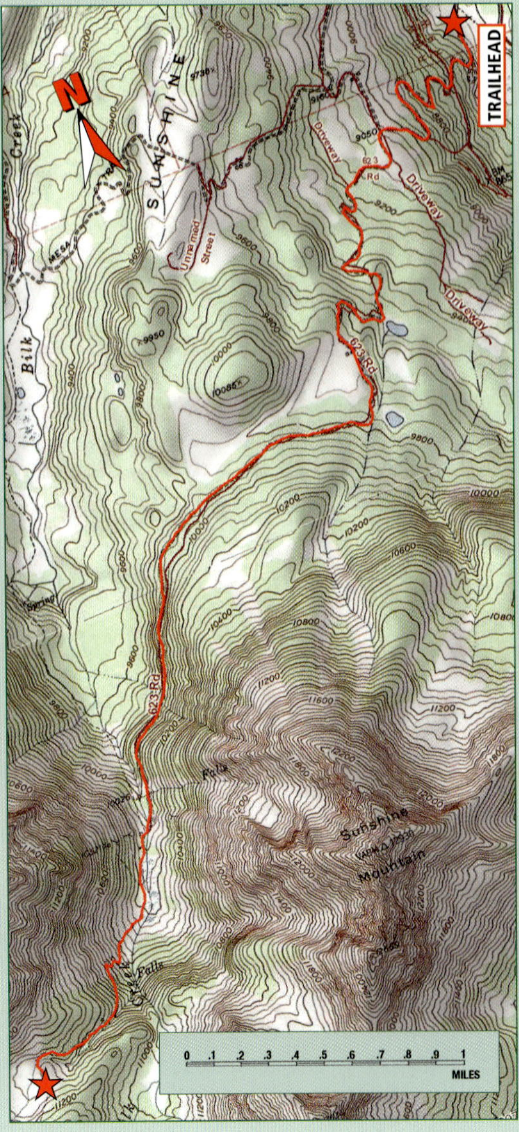
TRAILHEAD
N
SUNSHINE
MESA
Bilk Creek
Unnamed Street
Driveway
623 Rd
Spring
Falls
Creek Falls
Sunshine Mountain
0 .1 .2 .3 .4 .5 .6 .7 .8 .9 1
MILES

5. Blaine Basin Trail

BY ROD MARTINEZ

MAPS	Trails Illustrated, Telluride/ Silverton/Ouray/Lake City, Number 141; USGS, Mount Sneffels 7.5 minute; Latitude 40, Telluride/Silverton/Ouray Trails
ELEVATION GAIN	1,800 feet
RATING	Moderate
ROUND-TRIP DISTANCE	6.4 miles
ROUND-TRIP TIME	4–5 hours
NEAREST LANDMARK	Mount Sneffels

COMMENT: Mount Sneffels is one of the most photographed Fourteeners in the San Juan Mountains. It also is a beautiful mountain that can be climbed from a number of routes. The most difficult route is a direct ascent of the North Face from Blaine Basin. The trail described here takes you to that basin, where you are face to face with Sneffels' dominating North Face. The sheer beauty of the basin, the wildflowers, and the rock pinnacles are worth the time and effort for this hike.

GETTING THERE: From downtown Ridgway, go 4.8 miles west on Colorado 62 and turn left onto Dallas Creek Road (Ouray County Road 7). Begin measuring from here as you continue on CR 7. At 0.4 mile, turn left, and at 2.1 miles, turn right. At 6.0 miles, you will go around a large curve where you will get a great view down the valley to the base of Mount Sneffels. At 7.0 miles, CR 7 turns into Forest Road 851. The last 2.0 miles become rougher but are passable by all vehicles. There are numerous camping spots as you approach the trailhead 9.0 miles from the beginning of Dallas Creek Road.

The North Face of Mount Sneffels towers over Blaine Basin.

PHOTO BY ROD MARTINEZ

THE ROUTE: The trail begins about 75 yards from an old gate at the end of FR 851. Register at the trailhead and begin the hike on the trail on your left. The trail to the right will take you into Blue Lakes Basin.

The trail begins as an ATV/OHV trail and is easy to follow for approximately the first mile. There is little elevation gain as you hike through stands of aspens and conifers and patches of wildflowers before you reach the first major stream crossing. It can be done by wading through Wilson Creek as you continue to follow the ATV trail. Alternately, follow the spur trail right before this crossing, which is marked by a large downed tree and rock cairns and passes through the trees on the right to two large logs strapped together to form a bridge over the creek. During times of high runoff, water might overrun this log bridge and two others farther up the trail, making them slippery.

Shortly after the first water crossing, the ATV trail separates from the hiking trail. Turn right and proceed uphill to the second water crossing. Three logs strapped together cover the deeper section of the creek, but during high water, the rest of this crossing will be conducted by rock hopping

High Thirteeners of the Sneffels Range are an impressive sight on the Blaine Basin Trail. PHOTO BY ROD MARTINEZ

and possibly wading through some rapidly flowing and cold water. Another 0.4 mile beyond this crossing you will come to the third and final water crossing. Because the logs are larger, this crossing should be easier than the previous one.

After another 0.3 mile, the trail once again divides. Turning left will take you to Trail #203, Wilson Creek. Turning right continues as Blaine Basin Trail #202, which has an elevation gain of approximately 800 feet in the next 0.9 mile. This final ascent is well worth the effort as you climb into the basin. Shortly after the trail divides, a spur trail leads to the base of a spectacular waterfall.

Three miles from the start of the hike, the view becomes a grand panorama as the basin opens up. Continue upward for the last 0.2 mile on steep switchbacks, where your eyes will be filled with the grandeur of Blaine Basin and Mount Sneffels' North Face.

As a reminder, the stream crossings can be tricky, especially during times of high runoff in late May through mid-August. Hiking this trail may be best in late summer or early fall.

Retrace your steps to the trailhead. Regretfully, the stream crossings do not get any easier going down the trail.

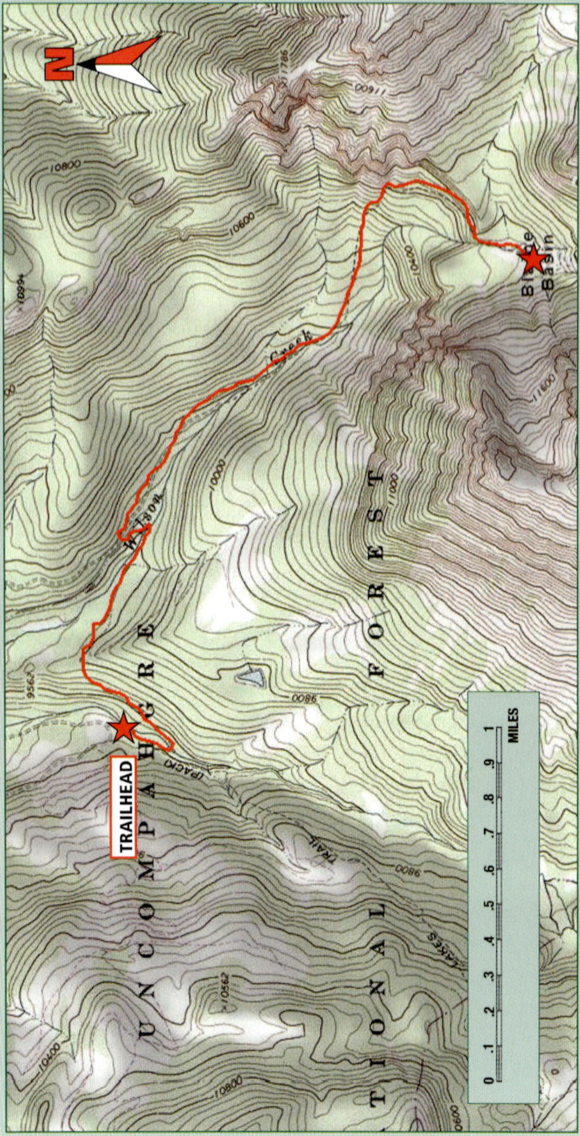

N
TRAILHEAD
Blaine Basin
UNCOMPAHGRE NATIONAL FOREST
Creek
(PACK) TRAIL
LAKES
10800
10600
10400
10000
9800
11000
11600
0 .1 .2 .3 .4 .5 .6 .7 .8 .9 1
MILES

6. Blue Lake Trail (Telluride)

BY JEFF EISELE

MAPS	Trails Illustrated, Telluride/ Silverton/Ouray/Lake City, Number 141; USGS, Telluride 7.5 minute; Latitude 40, Telluride/ Silverton/Ouray Trails
ELEVATION GAIN	2,020 feet to Blue Lake; 2,330 feet to Mud Lake
RATING	Moderate
ROUND-TRIP DISTANCE	5.6 miles to Blue Lake; 7.6 miles to Mud Lake
ROUND-TRIP TIME	3–4 hours to Blue Lake; 5–7 hours to Mud Lake
NEAREST LANDMARK	Bridal Veil Falls

COMMENT: One of the many Colorado lakes sharing this name (including another in this book), this Blue Lake is nestled beneath several unnamed Thirteeners high in East Basin above Bridal Veil Falls near Telluride. The trail follows an old mining road all the way to the lake. Along the way, you'll pass numerous waterfalls, as well as the remains of mining structures dating back to the late 1800s.

A prehike bonus is the drive from the Pandora Mill to the Bridal Veil Falls power plant adjacent to the rim of the 365-foot falls, affording stunning views of the falls along the way. And yet another bonus, if you desire, is extending your hike another mile to visit nearby Mud Lake.

GETTING THERE: From downtown Telluride, drive east through town on Colorado Avenue. Pass the old Pandora Mill and switchback up the side of the valley to a rough, rocky road to the top of Bridal Veil Falls and the power plant. Park at the switchback near the top of the falls, just before the road becomes one-way at 10,200 feet. It is 2.4 miles long with a

Hikers pass the remains of a number of old mining buildings and water lines as they near Blue Lake. PHOTO BY JEFF EISELE

1,200-foot elevation gain from the mill to the parking area. Because of the rough road those with passenger cars may want to walk the road instead of driving it.

THE ROUTE: Go through a gate advising hikers to stay on trail and pass to the left of and above the power plant. The trail travels almost due south for the first 1.2 miles on the east side of Bridal Veil Creek, passing the junction with the Silver Lake Trail after 0.4 mile. Numerous waterfalls cascade down the valley as you make your way up the basin. An unnamed 12,825-foot peak becomes more prominent as you hike through this section. It is at the end of the northern end of the ridge separating Bridal Veil and East basins.

At 1.2 miles, a short series of switchbacks takes you eastward up a slope, and then the trail turns south again. At 1.7 miles, another trail goes south into Bridal Veil Basin; stay left on the Blue Lake Trail, which curves around to the northeast for 0.2 mile to a point near the Royal Mine. Here an unnamed trail leads north, but the Blue Lake Trail switchbacks south. Follow it the remaining 0.9 mile to the lake. The trail tops out at 12,220 feet above the lake's northern shore.

Approaching Mud Lake, the connecting trail goes through a cleft in the small cliff band to the right of this waterfall.

PHOTO BY JEFF EISELE

The lake sits in a basin surrounded on three sides by Three Needles (13,481 feet) to the east and several other unnamed summits above 13,000 feet.

Return via the same route, or extend your hike 1.0 mile around the ridge east of Blue Lake into Mud Lake Basin. Descend 0.2 mile from Blue Lake and find an unmarked connecting trail on the lower slopes of the ridge. Contour around the ridge, staying close to the bottom of the cliffs; the trail is indistinct at best along this section.

As you round the ridge, the terrain becomes rockier and the way becomes more clear as the trail turns east. About 0.2 mile before reaching Mud Lake, you'll see a waterfall and a talus slope with a clear path going across it. Scramble up a short cleft in a small cliff band on the right side of the waterfall, and emerge in a grassy area with bushes just below the lake, which is at 12,250 feet.

It's worth taking a few minutes to hike around the south side of the lake to the upper part of the basin. It offers a beautiful view of the distant peaks of the Mount Sneffels Wilderness to the northwest, seemingly floating on the surface of Mud Lake.

Return to the Blue Lake Trail the way you came.

An elaborate cairn sits above the northern shore of Blue Lake. Several unnamed Thirteeners surround the lake.

PHOTO BY JEFF EISELE

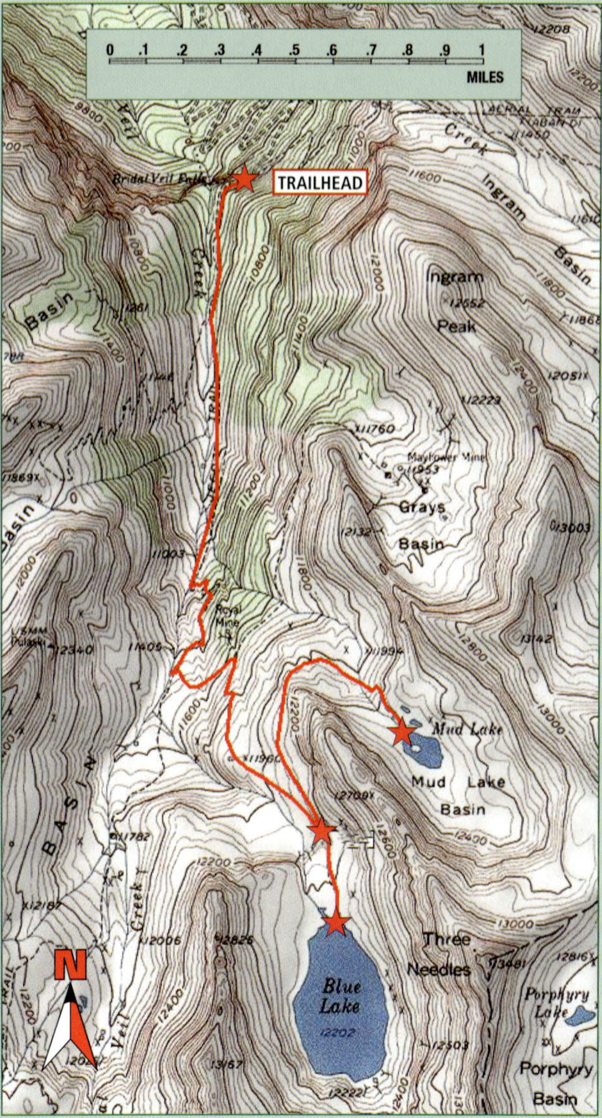
0 .1 .2 .3 .4 .5 .6 .7 .8 .9 1
MILES
TRAILHEAD
Bridal Veil Falls
Ingram Basin
Ingram Peak
12652
Creek
Basin
Mayflower Mine
Grays Basin
Royal Mine
Mud Lake
Mud Lake Basin
Blue Lake
12202
Three Needles
Porphyry Lake
Porphyry Basin
Veil Creek
BASIN
TRAIL
N

7. Blue Lakes Trail (Ridgway)

BY ROD MARTINEZ

MAPS	Trails Illustrated, Telluride/Silverton/Ouray/Lake City, Number 141; USGS, Mount Sneffels 7.5 minute; Latitude 40, Telluride/Silverton/Ouray Trails
ELEVATION GAIN	1,720 feet
RATING	Moderate
ROUND-TRIP DISTANCE	6.6 miles
ROUND-TRIP TIME	4–6 hours
NEAREST LANDMARK	Mount Sneffels

COMMENT: Mount Sneffels often is referred to as the Queen of the San Juan Mountains. Blue Lakes Basin is where all her turquoise jewelry is on display. This hike takes the trail to Lower Blue Lake, where the wildflowers from mid-July to the end of August are the crown jewels. The Blue Lakes Trail continues to the top of Blue Lakes Pass and eventually the summit of Mount Sneffels. Our destination is Lower Blue Lake.

GETTING THERE: From downtown Ridgway, go 4.8 miles west on Colorado 62 and turn left onto Dallas Creek Road (Ouray County Road 7). Begin measuring from here, as you continue on CR 7. At 0.4 mile, take a left, then at 2.1 miles take a right. At 6.0 miles, you will go around a large curve where you will get a great view down the valley to the base of Mount Sneffels. At 7.0 miles, CR 7 turns into Forest Road 851. The last 2 miles become rougher, but are passable by all vehicles. There are numerous camping spots as you approach the trailhead 9 miles from the beginning of Dallas Creek Road.

Wildflowers adorn the slopes above Lower Blue Lake.

PHOTO BY ROD MARTINEZ

THE ROUTE: The trail begins about 75 yards from an old gate at the end of Forest Road 851. Register at the trailhead and begin your hike on the trail on your right. The trail to the left will take you into Blaine Basin.

The Blue Lakes Trail follows along the side of the East Fork of Dallas Creek for a short distance before heading up the west side of a steep valley. Initially, parts of the trail are steep as you make your way through a thick forest of Engelmann spruce with occasional stands of tall aspens.

About 1.5 miles into the hike, you will cross a stream and enter another small but steep valley. The streambed in the center of the valley is an avalanche chute where occasional torrents of snow gather speed as they descend the steep slopes of the surrounding mountains. When there is a break in the forest, take time to admire Mount Sneffels. Her dignity rises above the high Thirteeners in the area.

The trail takes a distinct turn to the left and continues to gain elevation, although not as rapidly as the section of the trail just completed. About 1.5 miles farther, you will

Mount Sneffels, the 14,150-foot "Queen of the San Juans," from the upper reaches of Blue Lakes Basin. PHOTO BY ROD MARTINEZ

return to the East Fork of Dallas Creek, where you will hear the roar of two waterfalls. The first one cascades over a multitude of rocks, but you can walk right to the edge of the stream to enjoy the view up close. The second waterfall is farther away and drops about 75 feet to the rocks and canyon below it. It is a sight to see, but it is difficult to hike close to the edge of this waterfall.

In about 0.25 mile, you will reach the banks of Lower Blue Lake, and you immediately will see how the lake acquired its name. Hike through wildflower heaven on the west side of the lake until you find a spot to sit down and soak in the scenery that surrounds you. Blue Lakes Basin is encircled by Dallas Peak, Gilpin Peak, and Mount Sneffels. Lower Blue Lake fills this magical, peaceful, and circular bowl with "blue" water.

If time permits and you still are feeling adventurous, hike an additional 2.2 miles round trip with an additional elevation gain of 900 feet to Middle and Upper Blue Lakes. Retrace your steps to the trailhead.

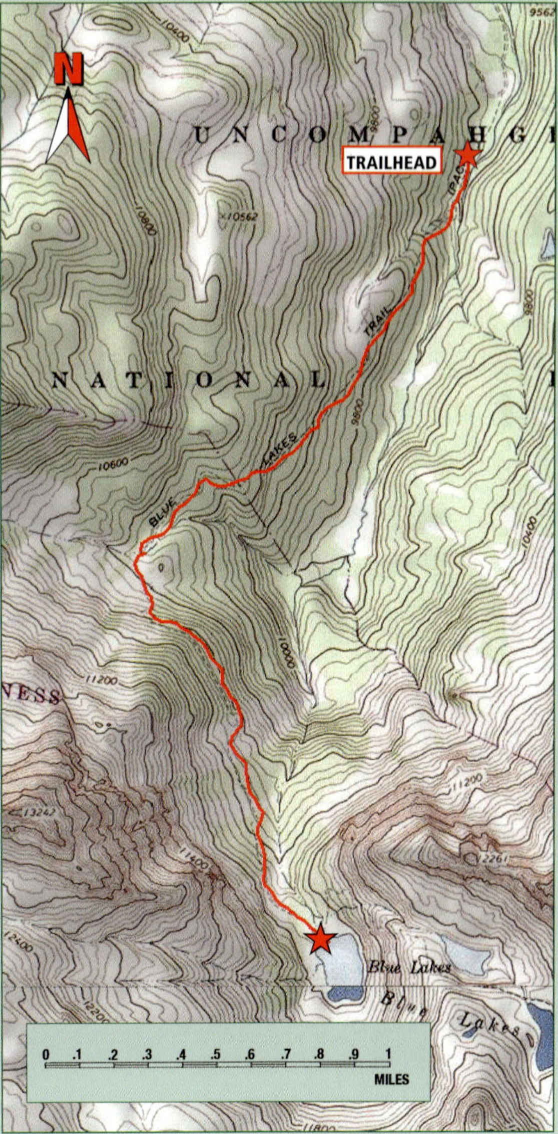
N
UNCOMPAHGRE
TRAILHEAD
NATIONAL
BLUE LAKES TRAIL
NESS
Blue Lakes
Blue Lakes
0 .1 .2 .3 .4 .5 .6 .7 .8 .9 1
MILES

8. Bridal Veil Falls Trail

BY ROD MARTINEZ

MAPS	Trails Illustrated, Telluride/ Silverton/Ouray/Lake City, Number 141; USGS, Telluride 7.5 minute; Latitude 40, Telluride/ Silverton/Ouray Trails
ELEVATION GAIN	1,200 feet
RATING	Easy to moderate
ROUND-TRIP DISTANCE	3.6 miles
ROUND-TRIP TIME	1.5–2.5 hours
NEAREST LANDMARK	Telluride

COMMENT: One of the iconic images of Telluride is of Bridal Veil Falls, situated in the box canyon at the east end of Telluride. This stunning waterfall is 365 feet long, the tallest free-falling falls in Colorado. It lures many people to hike, bike, or four-wheel drive up the road to the top of the waterfalls next to the prominent old power plant. The plant was built in 1907 to power the Smuggler-Union Mine 2,000 feet below, providing the first alternating current used for industrial purposes in the United States. It operated in its original configuration until 1953. The house/power plant atop the falls was restored in 1991 and operated and lived in until 2010. The power generated now provides about 25 percent of Telluride's demand for electricity. It is the second-oldest operating AC generator in the United States.

Bridal Veil Falls is a two-pronged waterfall. Please take notice that the plant now is private property, but you can walk around the outskirts and look in a westerly direction over the town of Telluride. The trail past the falls continues on to mountain meadows and lakes above 10,000 feet.

Bridal Veil Falls plunges from cliffs at the top of the box canyon east of Telluride. PHOTO BY ROD MARTINEZ

GETTING THERE: From the center of Telluride, travel east on Colorado Avenue for 2.0 miles, where you will go past the Pandora Mill. Park in the lot on the southeast side of the road. Arriving early will get you a spot in the lot. Otherwise you may have to park on the shoulder of the road.

THE ROUTE: This hike is easy to moderate as long as you are acclimated to the altitude.

It begins at an altitude of 9,000 feet. The top of the falls is at 10,200 feet for a gain of 1,200 feet.

From the parking lot, hike up the dirt road to the base of the waterfalls. The road is rocky and dusty but a very easy hike. Be aware of vehicle traffic. The road eventually turns into a one-way road from Red Mountain Pass over Black Bear Pass traveling from east to west. The turnaround point for vehicles is at the small parking area at the top of the waterfalls by the old power plant.

Take your time hiking the 1.2 miles to the base of the falls. As you work your way to the edge of the falls, you might be sprayed with water and the roar will overwhelm you as the

The historic power plant sits atop a cliff at the edge of Bridal Veil Falls.
PHOTO BY ROD MARTINEZ

water plunges from 365 feet above you to the boulders near your feet. In the early spring when the snow is melting around you, the flowing water is spectacular.

The top of the waterfall and the old power plant is another 0.6 mile. There is a gate across the old road as it goes up into higher destinations, such as hikes to Blue Lake and Silver Lake, as described in this pack guide.

At the top you will get a terrific view of the old power plant. It is amazing to consider how it was built and maintained on the side of the mountain—almost as amazing as the scenery that keeps unfolding before you as you hike up the trail. The box canyon walls seem impenetrable. The colors of the rocks and walls are enhanced in the fall when the aspens change color, giving you another form of gold all around.

Extending your hike 0.8 mile up the road toward Black Bear Pass brings you to Ingram Falls. Look down valley to the west into the town of Telluride. The zigzag road you hiked up now unfolds beneath you.

The 365-foot Bridal Veil Falls is the longest free-falling waterfall in Colorado. PHOTO BY ROD MARTINEZ

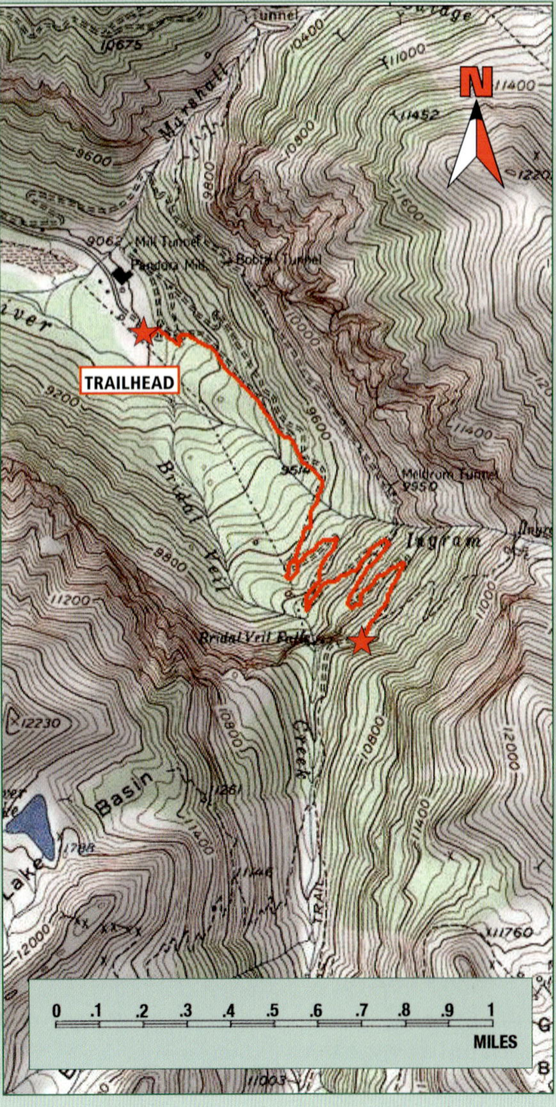
N
TRAILHEAD
Bridal Veil Falls
Bridal Veil
Creek
Ingram
Marshall
Mill Tunnel
Pandora Mill
Bobtail Tunnel
Meldrum Tunnel
Basin
Lake
TRAIL
0 .1 .2 .3 .4 .5 .6 .7 .8 .9 1
MILES

9. Courthouse Mountain Trail

BY SANDY HOAGLAND

MAPS	Trails Illustrated, Telluride/Silverton/Ouray/Lake City, Number 141; USGS, Courthouse Mountain 7.5 minute; Latitude 40, Southwest Colorado Trails
ELEVATION GAIN	1,800 feet
RATING	Moderate/Difficult because of rapid elevation gain
ROUND-TRIP DISTANCE	3.7 miles
ROUND-TRIP TIME	3–4 hours
NEAREST LANDMARK	Ridgway

COMMENT: Courthouse Mountain (12,152 feet) is an impressive peak with sheer cliffs that drop dramatically from its grassy, rock-topped summit. Viewed from Ridgway, this peak looks like a challenging technical climb, but the approach from the east basically is a walk-up. Though it is a steep climb, it is only 1.8 miles to the summit on a well-defined trail. The last 500 feet of elevation gets steeper and requires some scrambling to get above a rock band, but the effort is rewarded with a fabulous 360-degree view atop this somewhat airy summit. For those who are deterred by the steepness or the scrambling, there are fine views to the north and east below the steepest stretch of trail, as well as interesting rock formations on the south side of the summit.

GETTING THERE: From the traffic light at the intersection of U.S. 550 and Colorado 62 in Ridgway, it is 18.9 miles to the trailhead, mostly on dirt roads. Following the signs to Owl Creek Pass covers the first 18.0 miles of the route. Start measuring mileage at the traffic light and travel 1.8 miles north on U.S. 550 to a right turn (east) on County Road 10. At 2.7 miles (from the traffic light), bear left toward

Courthouse Mountain appears to be a tough climb, but the trail to the summit, though steep, is basically a walk-up. PHOTO BY SANDY HOAGLAND

Owl Creek Pass and Silver Jack Reservoir, staying on CR 10. At 4.5 miles, continue straight on CR 10. At 6.0 miles, bear right on CR 8. Views of Courthouse Mountain and Chimney Rock now are visible. Go left at 7.5 miles, staying on CR 8. The Uncompahgre National Forest boundary is at mile 10, where the road becomes Forest Road 858. Bear left again at 11 miles. Continue on FR 858 to Owl Creek Pass at 17.0 miles. At 17.3 miles, take a right onto FR 860. Follow it for 1.6 miles to the trailhead, which is well marked on the right, with ample parking on the left side of the road.

THE ROUTE: The trailhead (Forest Service Trail #218) is well marked. After crossing a bridge, the ascent begins, and the trail maintains a fairly consistent grade for most of the first 0.8 mile. At this point, Trail 218 continues into the Uncompahgre Wilderness (beyond the Wilderness boundary sign), but the trail to Courthouse Mountain summit splits off to the right (northwest). A sign indicates it is 1.0 mile to the summit.

Take the trail to the summit. You will soon see dramatic overlooks of interesting volcanic rock formations from the

Blazing fall colors light up the mountainside on Owl Creek Pass along the drive to the Courthouse Mountain Trailhead. PHOTO BY SANDY HOAGLAND

left side of the ridge. The views get even better farther up the trail. As you continue climbing, stay on the new trail, which has convenient switchbacks through the trees, and ignore the old, steeper trail that climbs straight up the grassy slope to the right.

Once at the ridge above, views of Chimney Rock appear to the north. The remaining route to the summit gets steeper, initially climbing up a dirt trail through the trees, followed by some scrambling up a short section of conglomerate rock. Beyond the rock is a short stretch of relatively stable talus, after which the trail returns to dirt through the last steep grassy stretch heading up to the summit.

The views from the summit are spectacular, including Chimney Rock, Cimarron Ridge, and Silver Jack Reservoir to the north; Turret Ridge, Dunsinane Mountain, Precipice Peak, Redcliff Peak, and Coxcomb Peak along the ridge to the east and southeast; Ouray and the Sneffels Range to the southwest; and Ridgway Reservoir to the northwest.

After enjoying the summit, return to the trailhead using the same route as your approach.

Chimney Rock dominates the vista from below.
PHOTO BY SANDY HOAGLAND

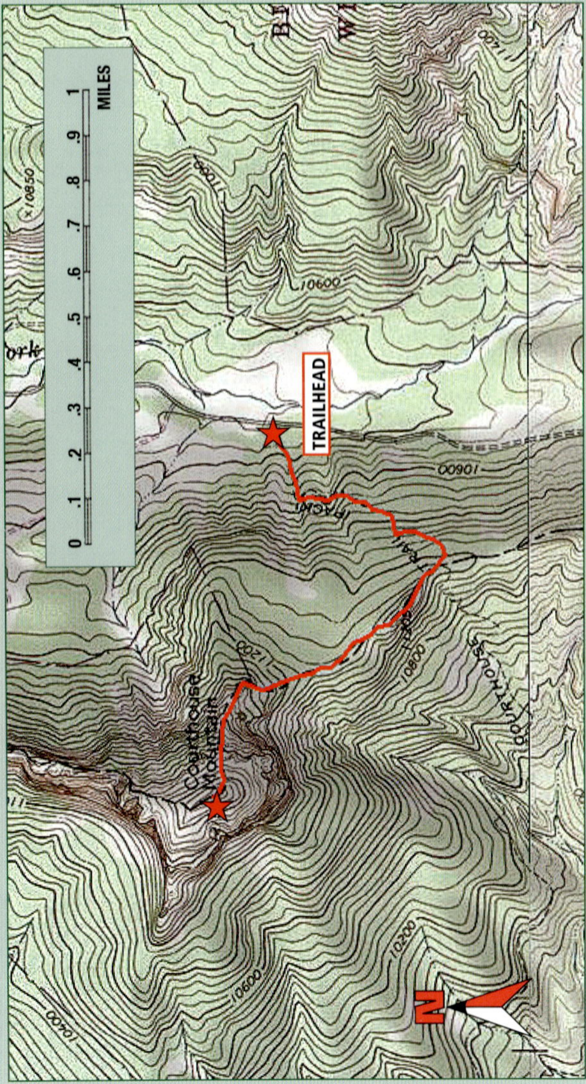
TRAILHEAD
Courthouse Mountain
0 .1 .2 .3 .4 .5 .6 .7 .8 .9 1
MILES
10600
10800
11200
10200
10400
N

10. Cross Mountain Trail

BY CHRISTIAN GREEN

MAPS	Trails Illustrated, Telluride/Silverton/Ouray/Lake City, Number 141; USGS, Mount Wilson 7.5 minute; Latitude 40, Telluride/Silverton/Ouray Trails
ELEVATION GAIN	1,900 feet
RATING	Moderate
ROUND-TRIP DISTANCE	6.6 miles
ROUND-TRIP TIME	5–6 hours
NEAREST LANDMARK	Lizard Head Pass

COMMENT: The Cross Mountain Trail is located within the 41,193-acre Lizard Head Wilderness, which was designated a wilderness area by Congress in 1980 through the Colorado Wilderness Act. Just 17 miles southwest of Telluride, the trailhead is easily accessible from Colorado 145.

The trail affords stunning views of several San Juan Fourteeners, including El Diente (14,159 feet), Mount Wilson (14,246), and Wilson Peak (14,017), all of which are west of the trail. In addition, Lizard Head, a 13,113-foot volcanic plug, becomes increasingly prominent as the trail climbs toward this monolith, the base of which is the terminus of the hike. Some people consider Lizard Head the most challenging climb in Colorado; it was not scaled until Albert R. Ellingwood and Barton Hoag accomplished the feat in 1920.

Although the area immediately around the trail is largely devoid of aspens, fall is a wonderful time of the year to explore this trail, especially when there is a light dusting of snow on the surrounding mountains.

GETTING THERE: From the "Society Turn" roundabout west of Telluride on Colorado 145, go south on 145 toward Rico.

The Cross Mountain Trail leads to the base of 13,113-foot Lizard Head, a spire considered by many to be Colorado's toughest climb.

PHOTO BY CHRISTIAN GREEN

The next few miles provide ample opportunity to soak in the breathtaking views of the aspens, especially during a crisp blue-colored sky day during the fall. This stretch of highway includes several turnouts that are great places to take pictures of the fall foliage and the mountains. Continue on for a few more miles until reaching Lizard Head Pass, which is about 15 miles from Telluride. At this point travel 2 more miles to the parking lot for the Cross Mountain Trailhead on the right. The turnoff can be tricky to spot, so keep your eyes peeled.

THE ROUTE: From the north side of the parking lot, the trailhead begins to the right of the Lizard Head Wilderness map at a small wooden bridge that fords a creek. The elevation at the trailhead is approximately 10,040 feet, and the route gradually climbs to just under 12,000 feet at the base of Lizard Head, where the trail ends as it connects with the Lizard Head Trail.

The first 0.5 mile of the trail is open as it gradually climbs toward a forest primarily composed of spruce and fir. Shortly after you pass the Groundhog Stock Trail

The Mount Wilson massif dominates the skyline to the west of the trail.
PHOTO BY CHRISTIAN GREEN

on the left, you enter a stretch of woods that lasts for about the next 1.5 miles. When the trail opens up again, Lizard Head is front and center, making it difficult for the hiker not to be transfixed by this unique spire that reaches toward the sky. With the destination now in clear sight, the ascent seemingly becomes easier, mainly due to the motivation of capturing a close-up photo of one of Colorado's unique monoliths.

During the next mile or so, the trail meanders toward Lizard Head through a sparse landscape—especially once you reach treeline—composed of rocks and very little vegetation until reaching the intersection with the Lizard Head Trail at the 3.3-mile mark. At this point, you are at the base of Lizard Head.

If you haven't already taken some time to admire Colorado's most unique Thirteener, grab your camera and get a few pictures of this striking San Juan spire before retracing your steps and heading back down the trail. On the way down, be sure to take in the Fourteeners to your right (west) and the high Thirteeners above Trout Lake to the east.

Gladstone Peak (13,913 feet), left, and 14,017-foot Wilson Peak rise prominently northwest of the trail.
PHOTO BY CHRISTIAN GREEN

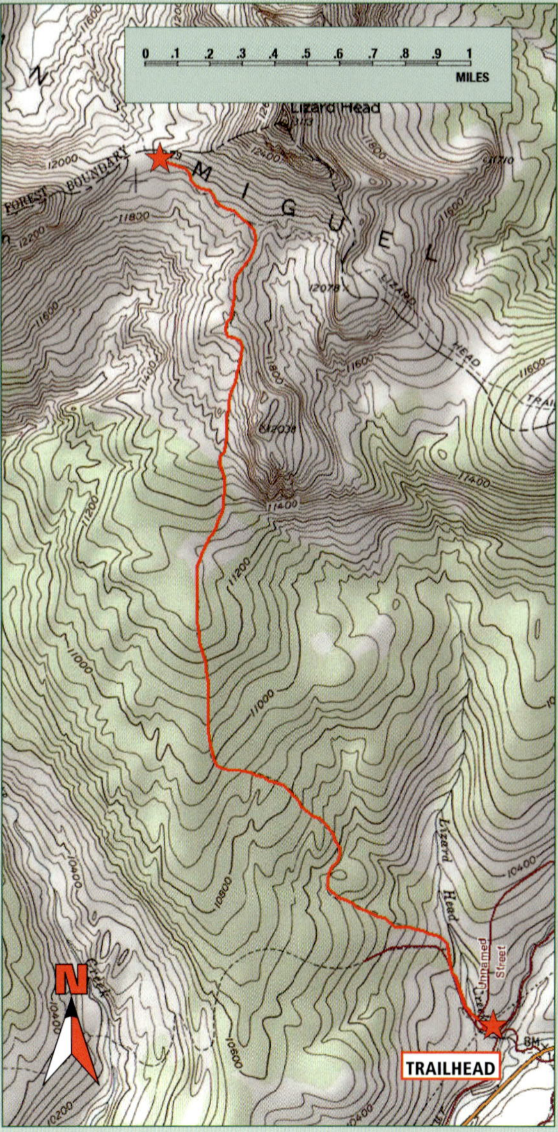
0 .1 .2 .3 .4 .5 .6 .7 .8 .9 1
MILES
Lizard Head
FOREST BOUNDARY
M I G U E L
LIZARD HEAD TRAIL
Lizard Head
Unnamed Street
TRAILHEAD
N

11. Kilpacker-Navajo Lake Trail

BY DIANA DONNELLY

MAPS	Trails Illustrated, Telluride/Silverton/Ouray/Lake City, Number 141; USGS, Dolores Peak 7.5 minute; Latitude 40, Telluride/Silverton/Ouray Trails
ELEVATION GAIN	1,400 feet
RATING	Moderate
ROUND-TRIP DISTANCE	12.2 miles
ROUND-TRIP TIME	6–7 hours
NEAREST LANDMARK	Lizard Head Pass

COMMENT: The Kilpacker and Navajo Lake trails are well-known and favorite hikes for locals, as well as those who often travel to this astounding area. The trails traverse a variety of beautiful terrain. The Navajo Lake Trail takes the adventurer to the surreal Navajo Lake, which is surrounded by the splendor of its alpine setting. Most sections of the trails are within the Lizard Head Wilderness Area, so wilderness guidelines apply. The forest road to the trailhead parking area is not plowed when there is snow.

GETTING THERE: From the "Society Turn" roundabout west of Telluride on Colorado 145, go south on 145 toward Lizard Head Pass. About 5.2 miles beyond the pass, Dunton Road (Forest Road 535) turns sharply off the highway to the right. (If you pass Cayton Campground on the left side of 145, you've gone too far.) This ascending, narrow, two-way, sometimes-rutted road winds around and comes to an open area—"The Meadows"—at about 3.5 miles. Continue past the turnoff for Eagle Peak Road on the left until you see a sign on the right for the Kilpacker Trailhead at 10,060 feet. Park here.

Majestic Gladstone Peak, one of Colorado's "Centennials," or highest 100 peaks, looks down on Navajo Lake. PHOTO BY DIANA DONNELLY

THE ROUTE: As the trail (#203) begins, there is a gentle rise through an array of summer wildflowers, including bluebells, mountain aster, wild iris, and wild clover. After a 100-foot elevation gain, you will see a sign marking a cutoff trail to the left to the main Navajo Lake Trailhead parking lot. Continue straight on the Kilpacker Trail.

Traveling through aspens, small meadows, and spruce/fir, you will get glimpses of Dolores Peak to the left until you arrive at the Lizard Head Wilderness sign at about 1.5 miles. The woods become denser with an abundance of forest lichen hanging from the trees. The forest is a playground for flickers and Clark's nutcrackers. The ground is spotted with nonpoisonous and poisonous mushrooms in late summer.

In another mile, you will arrive at the climbers' trail leading to the summit of El Diente. Only experienced climbers should attempt scaling this Fourteener. Proceed on the Kilpacker Trail as it descends slightly and crosses the swelling Kilpacker Creek. After some small ups and downs, the

El Diente (14,159 feet) is an imposing sight from the Kilpacker Trailhead.
PHOTO BY ROD MARTINEZ

trail descends about 200 feet while switchbacking to the swiftly running West Dolores River. On the other side of the river, you ascend slightly to the intersection with the Navajo Lake Trail (#635).

Turn right (north). After more gentle ascents through patches of forest and meadows, there is a magnificent view of falls on the West Dolores, framed by tall wildflowers. Soon after, you ascend more abruptly and switchback up forest hillsides before arriving at grassy slopes mixed with scree. This might feel like a challenge to some because of the elevation. At 11,400 feet, the trail arrives at the intersection with the Woods Lake Trail.

Veer right and continue another 0.75 mile to Navajo Lake, passing through rocky areas, some colonized by pika, and sections of krummholz. You can hear the roar of the river as the trail winds through the head of Navajo Basin. There are wilderness campsites for backpackers on both sides of the trail before it arrives at the headwaters of the West Dolores at 11,154 feet. Here you have an unrestricted view of the glacier cirque: the panorama of Navajo Lake surrounded by the majestic high peaks, including El Diente, Gladstone Peak, and Mount Wilson.

This hike ends here—the lake is a good spot for reflection and lunch—but the trail continues on the left side of the lake to junctions with the Silver Pick and Bilk Creek trails and climbers' routes to nearby summits.

Retrace your steps to the trailhead. Be mindful of the slippery scree slopes on your way down.

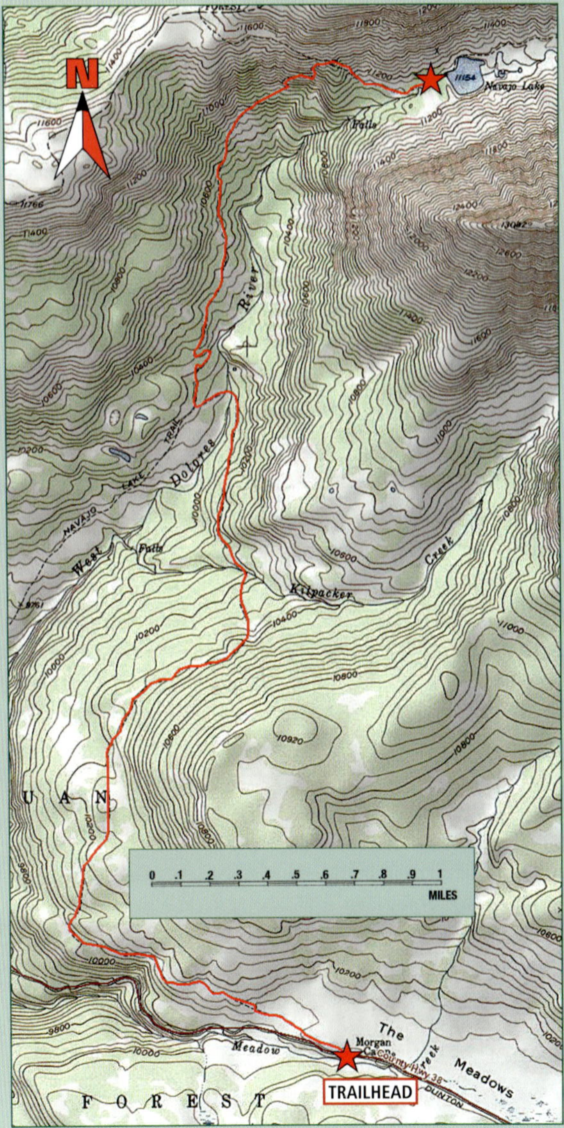
N
Navajo Lake
11154
Falls
River
Dolores
West
Falls
NAVAJO LAKE TRAIL
Kilpacker
Creek
13082
10920
U A N
F O R E S T
0 .1 .2 .3 .4 .5 .6 .7 .8 .9 1
MILES
The Meadows
Meadow
Morgan
County Hwy 38
DUNTON
TRAILHEAD

12. Lake Hope Trail

BY LASZLO SZUECS

MAPS	Trails Illustrated, Telluride/ Silverton/Ouray/Lake City, Number 141; USGS, Ophir 7.5 minute; Latitude 40, Telluride/ Silverton/Ouray Trails
ELEVATION GAIN	1,100 feet
RATING	Moderate
ROUND-TRIP DISTANCE	5.0 miles
ROUND-TRIP TIME	3–5 hours
NEAREST LANDMARK	Lizard Head Pass

COMMENT: Gorgeous mountain scenery and proximity to Telluride make this one of the most popular hikes in the Telluride area. The hike can be extended to gain even more scenic views. The best time of year for this hike is late June through early October. Experienced snowshoe hikers can complete the hike during the winter but expect some route-finding problems and steep switchbacks. If you are up to this snowshoe challenge, the view of the snowcapped mountains is as spectacular as the fields of wildflowers in the summer.

GETTING THERE: From the "Society Turn" roundabout on Colorado 145 west of Telluride, go south (toward Dolores) 10.1 miles and turn left at the Trout Lake turnoff (identified first by a yellow Trout Lake highway sign, then by a brown sign reading "National Forest Access—Priest Lake"). The Trout Lake turnoff is 8.5 miles from the Mountain Village exit. If you are coming from Dolores, it is 1.9 miles after Lizard Head Pass.

After 0.2 mile on the Trout Lake road, the road to Priest Lake will branch off to the left, but you will continue on the road along Trout Lake past numerous private cottages.

Lake Hope and Peak V8 viewed from the west. PHOTO BY LAURA SCULL

At 1.7 miles from the highway, soon after entering national forest land, you will come to a road junction at a tree in the middle of a meadow. As advised by a sign at the junction, turn left to proceed to the Lake Hope Trailhead.

If you are interested in historical artifacts, take a short detour: Before taking the turn at the road junction, drive straight for 500 feet to a historical site, an old railroad trestle. The road around Trout Lake follows the path of the Galloping Goose railroad grade of mining days past.

From the road junction at the tree, it's another 2.5 miles to the trailhead at 10,760 feet on a sometimes-bumpy road (a high-clearance vehicle is highly recommended). Parking at the trailhead is limited; if you do not arrive at the crack of dawn, you might have to park along the road.

THE ROUTE: Soon after the trailhead, the trail crosses the creek in Poverty Gulch. In spring, the snow bridge above the trail might be the best place to cross the creek.

The trail doesn't gain any elevation through the first half of the hike to Lake Hope. Toward the end of the first half you will cross a few minor creeks in a sparsely wooded area and

Lake Fork stream and San Miguel Peak as seen from the Lake Hope Trail. PHOTO BY LASZLO SZUECS

come to a wooden sign that reassures you of being on the Lake Hope Trail. At this point the trail starts to climb to timberline through many switchbacks and finally levels out over the homestretch to the lake at 11,840 feet, where you will be ready to absorb the spectacular scenery around you.

Conditions permitting, you might want to extend the hike for even better views of mountains and wildflowers. One option is to continue on the trail to the 12,445-foot saddle southeast of the lake, with views of San Miguel Peak to the west, Rolling Mountain to the southeast, and Twin Sisters to the east. Another option is to hike to the north end of the lake (over or counterclockwise around the knoll on the northeast side of the lake). From the dam at the north end of the lake, you can hike in moderate terrain to the lush meadows of wildflowers above the steep terrain on the west side of the lake. You will have good views of the mountains to the northeast, dominated by 13,894-foot Vermilion Peak.

After restoring your spirit at the lake, retrace your steps to the trailhead.

Pilot Knob (left) and Vermilion Peak (center) dominate the skyline from the meadows above Lake Hope. PHOTO BY LASZLO SZUECS

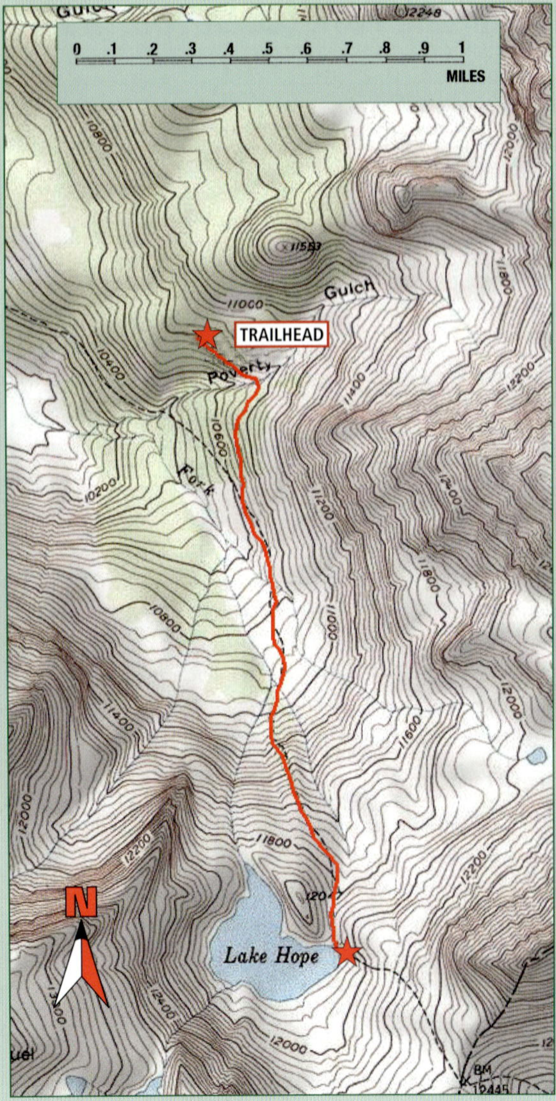

LAKE HOPE TRAIL

13. Middle Fork (Cimarron) Trail

BY JEFF EISELE

MAPS	Trails Illustrated, Telluride/ Silverton/Ouray/Lake City, Number 141; USGS, Courthouse Mountain and Wetterhorn Peak 7.5 minute; Latitude 40, Southwest Colorado Trails
ELEVATION GAIN	1,600 feet
RATING	Moderate
ROUND-TRIP DISTANCE	8.6 miles
ROUND-TRIP TIME	4–6 hours
NEAREST LANDMARK	Silver Jack Reservoir

COMMENT: The Middle Fork Trail (#227) travels south along the Middle Fork of the Cimarron River, which bisects ridgelines on each side with dramatic spires and peaks, many higher than 12,000 feet. The trail stays close to the river for the length of this description, traveling through pine forest and giving way to high alpine meadows. In July and August, hikers are ushered all the way with a beautiful array of wildflowers. The ascent is remarkably consistent throughout with an easy, gradual grade.

GETTING THERE: Measure from the traffic light in Ridgway (intersection of U.S. 550 and Colorado 62). Travel 1.8 miles north on U.S. 550 and turn right (east) on County Road 10. At 2.7 miles, bear left, staying on CR 10 and following the signs to Owl Creek Pass and Silver Jack Reservoir. At 4.5 miles, continue straight on CR 10. At 6.0 miles, bear right on CR 8. Courthouse Mountain and Chimney Rock now come into view to the southeast. Go left at 7.5 miles, staying on CR 8. The Uncompahgre National Forest boundary is at mile 10, where the road becomes Forest Road 858. Bear left again at 11.0 miles, and continue on FR 858 to Owl Creek

Precipice Peak as seen during the first mile on the Middle Fork of the Cimarron Trail. PHOTO BY JEFF EISELE

Pass at 17.0 miles. At 17.3 miles, continue left on FR 858. At 24.1 miles, turn right on FR 861, and follow it to the end of the road and the trailhead at 28.8 miles (go straight at the intersection with FR 861B on your right at 26.0 miles). Elevation at the trailhead is 10,300 feet.

THE ROUTE: The trail begins on the right side of the parking area as you drive in. Sign the trail register and follow a short, stone-lined path along the banks of the rocky riverbed that leads you onto the trail.

The trail ascends gradually through the trees, hugging the creek at the outset. After 0.9 mile, you'll reach a marshy meadow, where logs and rocks have been placed to help keep your boots dry for the short walk through the grass and back into the forest.

Go straight at 2.3 miles, where the Porphyry Basin Trail branches to the left, and cross the creek just below a little gorge. Here, you'll arrive at one of the few places along the way where the grade gets notably steeper, but it's a short, 0.1-mile section with a couple switchbacks leading into an area where views of the surrounding peaks begin to open

With Coxcomb Peak looming above, hikers near timberline at the head of the basin on the Middle Fork of the Cimarron Trail. PHOTO BY JEFF EISELE

up. Hikers have to maneuver around some downed timber in this section, but the few obstacles are not difficult and the rest of the trail is mostly clear.

At 3.0 miles, you can walk a short distance right of the trail for a view of some falls upriver. Soon after that, the trail reaches a large meadow affording a view into the upper reaches of the basin, where you'll see Redcliff and Coxcomb peaks on the west side of the basin and a couple of unnamed Thirteeners at the head of the basin.

You'll hike up another short, steeper section leading to another meadow higher in the basin. The first of a series of wood posts marking the higher sections of the trail is at 3.3 miles. This description ends just below timberline at 4.3 miles and an elevation of 11,630 feet, where the trail turns east and begins to climb more steeply to a 12,595-foot saddle.

If time, weather conditions, and energy permit, the remaining 1.2 miles and 970-foot climb to the saddle are well worth it for the view south of two Fourteeners, Uncompahgre (14,309) and Wetterhorn (14,015) peaks, and Matterhorn Peak (13,590) between them. Wood posts mark the trail to the saddle.

Retrace your steps to return to the trailhead.

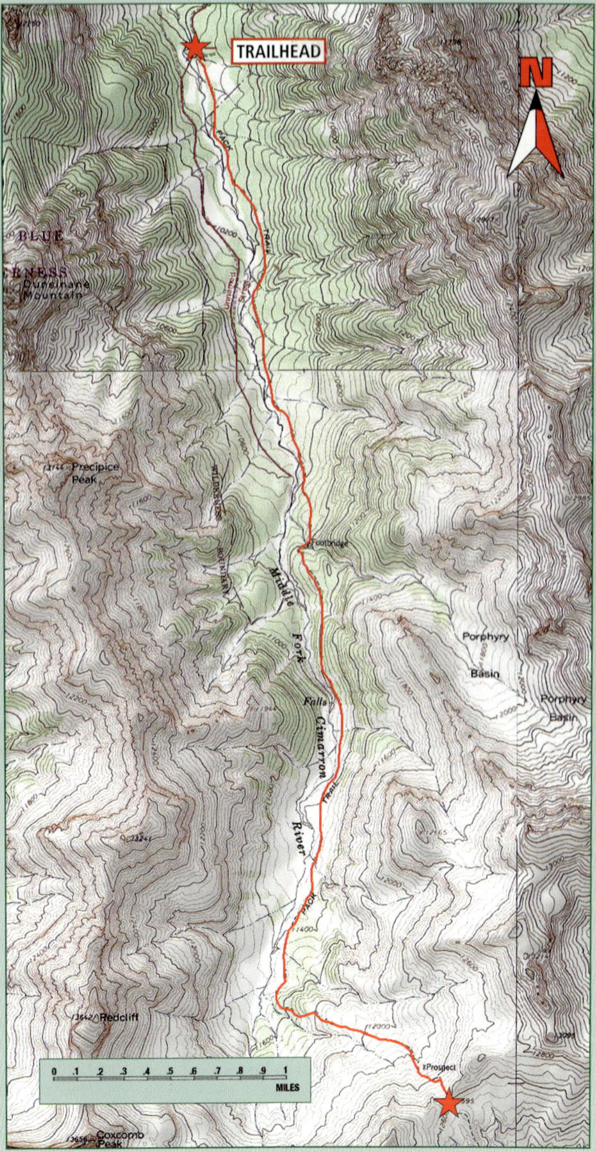

TRAILHEAD
N
BLUE
NESS
Dunsinane Mountain
Precipice Peak
WILDERNESS BOUNDARY
Footbridge
Middle Fork Cimarron River
Falls
Trail
Porphyry Basin
Porphyry Basin
Redcliff
Coxcomb Peak
Prospect
0 .1 .2 .3 .4 .5 .6 .7 .8 .9 1
MILES

14. San Miguel River Trail

BY ROD MARTINEZ

MAPS	Trails Illustrated, Telluride/Silverton/Ouray/Lake City, Number 141; USGS, Telluride 7.5 minute; Latitude 40, Telluride/Silverton/Ouray Trails
ELEVATION GAIN	170 feet
RATING	Easy
ROUND-TRIP DISTANCE	1–6 miles
ROUND-TRIP TIME	1–3 hours
NEAREST LANDMARK	Telluride

COMMENT: Like a number of towns in western Colorado, Telluride is best known as a "ski town." Besides skiing, though, Telluride has a lot to offer the rest of the year. In the fall, the walls of the box canyon that surround Telluride turn to gold as the aspens finish their annual ritual of changing colors. The spring and summer seasons reveal an abundance of wildflowers and an array of impressive waterfalls. For a great view of Telluride and the surrounding area, take a ride on the gondola to Mountain Village and then ride back down to Telluride. The trip is free except during ski season, but the views of the surrounding 14,000-foot snowcapped mountains that surround you are priceless.

As you enter Telluride, you will feel like you are going back in time to when mining, not skiing, was the mainstay. The center of town still looks much like it did in the 1880s. Today, Telluride is designated as a National Historic Landmark. The old brick hotels and clapboard storefronts make for a pleasant and unique walk along the San Miguel River Trail.

An early morning reflection in the river along the San Miguel River Trail in Telluride. PHOTO BY ROD MARTINEZ

GETTING THERE: The trail can be accessed from almost anywhere in Telluride. Paid parking is limited. A second option is to continue east on Colorado Avenue past Pine Street to Telluride Town Park, where there is plenty of parking and restrooms. Even this parking becomes harder to find as the day progresses. An early start is advisable, so you can park at the park or near the gondola at the corner of Aspen Street and San Juan Avenue.

THE ROUTE: The San Miguel River Trail runs the length of Telluride and gains only 170 feet in elevation. The town's official elevation is 8,750 feet. The trail is perfect to help become acclimated to the elevation you will experience on moderate or more difficult trails in the surrounding area. It is dog-friendly, as well as a hiking, walking, jogging, and biking path.

Starting in the center of town and hiking east, you will have slight ups and downs on the trail as you head toward the Pandora Mine and the trailhead for Bridal Veil Falls. A short loop, less than a mile, can be made by starting on the south side of the San Miguel River at the Bear Creek Falls Trailhead. You then walk by a group of beaver ponds, the Fred Shellman Memorial Stage, Hanley Pavilion, and the

Passing a small pond walking east toward the Pandora Mine on the San Miguel River Trail. PHOTO BY ROD MARTINEZ

other amenities of Town Park. In about 100 yards, you will cross back over the San Miguel River, where you can turn back west and walk along the north side of the river to your starting point.

Instead of turning west, you can continue east along the trail on the north side of the river to the Pandora Mine and an unobstructed view of Bridal Veil Falls. The round-trip distance from the Bear Creek Trailhead to the Pandora Mine is approximately 4.5 miles.

Another alternative is to hike west from the Bear Creek Trailhead. This part of the trail also is a well-maintained, graded, level path. After 2.0 miles, the trail intersects with the Boomerang Trail, a steep 1.0-mile trail to Mountain Village. At this intersection, you can cross the bridge, where you will connect with the paved bike path that makes for a nice loop back to Telluride.

Whatever direction you are hiking, you will be alongside the San Miguel River, one of only two free-flowing rivers in Colorado. The running water, mixture of flowers, and historic homes make for a nice hike.

Wildflowers color your walk on the San Miguel River Trail. PHOTO BY ROD MARTINEZ

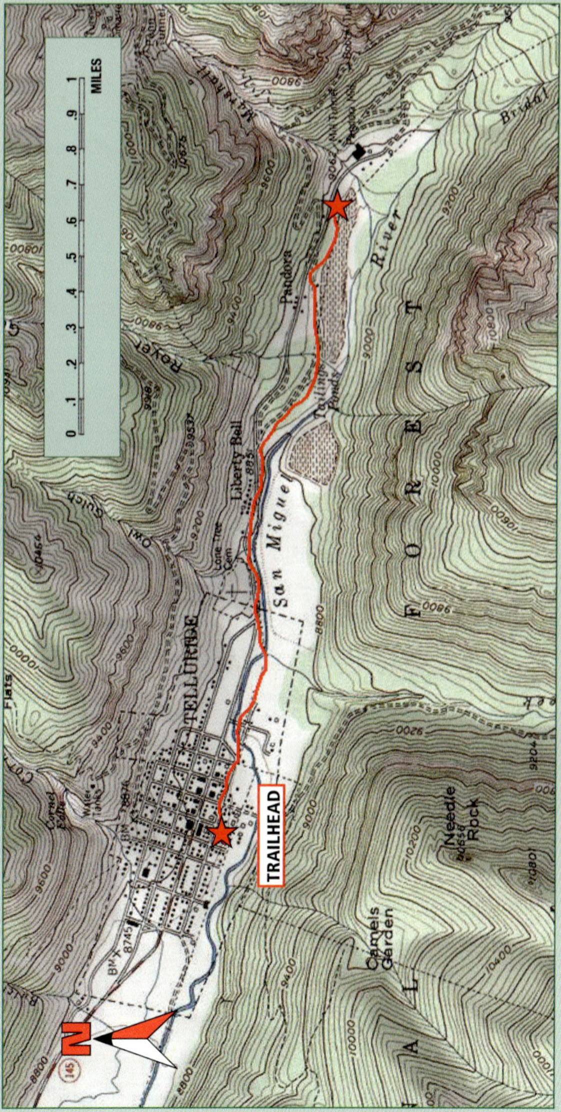
TRAILHEAD
TELLURIDE
San Miguel
River
Pandora
Liberty Bell
Tailings Ponds
Needle Rock
Camels Garden
Owl Gulch
Royer
Cornet Falls
Bridal
F O R E S T
MILES
0 .1 .2 .3 .4 .5 .6 .7 .8 .9 1
N
145

15. Silver Lake Trail

BY LAURA SCULL

MAPS	Trails Illustrated, Telluride/ Silverton/Ouray/Lake City, Number 141; USGS, Telluride 7.5 minute; Latitude 40, Telluride/ Silverton/Ouray Trails
ELEVATION GAIN	1,670 feet
RATING	Difficult
ROUND-TRIP DISTANCE	3.2 miles
ROUND-TRIP TIME	2–4 hours
NEAREST LANDMARK	Bridal Veil Falls

COMMENT: Silver Lake is a short but steep hike above Bridal Veil Falls popular with local hikers, fishermen, and campers. The lake is nestled in a beautiful alpine meadow with many possibilities for exploring above and around it. The trail is short but very steep and difficult in spots, so this destination is best for experienced hikers.

GETTING THERE: From downtown Telluride, drive east through town on Colorado Avenue. Pass the old Pandora Mill and switchback up the side of the valley to a rough, rocky road to the top of Bridal Veil Falls and the power plant. Park at the switchback near the top of the falls, just before the road becomes one-way. It is 2.4 miles long with a 1,200-foot elevation gain from the mill to the parking area. Those with passenger cars may want to walk the road.

THE ROUTE: Pass through the gate and start walking up the road, which runs above the falls and the power plant. At 0.4 mile, follow an obvious path that leaves the road to the west and hop across the creek on rocks at a wide, shallow spot. From here, the real work begins.

Silver Lake is nestled at the base of Peak 13,145 and Ballard Mountain to the west. PHOTO BY LAURA SCULL

The trail goes directly up the hillside after the creek crossing, trending first left and then right at an intersection. It is overgrown in spots but is easy to follow. It switchbacks steeply, passing through several small bands of rock that might require a little scrambling. You soon will find yourself zigzagging up an open hillside, looking down on the road and the creek in the valley below.

After climbing steadily for about half an hour, the trail starts trending north toward the ridgeline and back into the trees, which provide welcome shade as you continue steeply upward. The trail is well-defined and easy to follow, but it is badly eroded in places and periodically crosses small rocky steps, so this is not a good place for novice hikers or those unsure of their footing. Sturdy hiking boots are recommended to provide better ankle support.

After more switchbacks, the trail leads around a corner to an open rocky area at about 11,400 feet. Stop here to catch your breath and watch the Jeeps and ATVs creep down the four-wheel-drive road from Bear Mountain, clearly visible across the valley. This road, Black Bear Pass, is reached from U.S. 550 south of Ouray. It is one-way downhill from the pass to just above the top of Bridal Veil Falls.

View from the ridge above the lake, looking down into Telluride.
PHOTO BY LAURA SCULL

The trail continues at a more moderate grade into an alpine basin above the trees. The views open up as you walk through the meadow, which is a great place to admire the wildflowers. One final rise of a couple hundred feet brings you to the edge of Silver Lake at 11,788 feet.

From the lake, there are many possibilities for exploring. Circle the lake and admire the view from all angles. Head up the slope to the south to explore the old mines or cross over into Jackass Basin. If you climb up the slope to the ridge northwest of the lake and follow it to the high point on the northeastern end at 12,230 feet, you will be rewarded with panoramic views into the Telluride valley and the mountains in all directions. Or spend your afternoon at the edge of the lake watching the fish as they swim through the clear water.

Once you've enjoyed the scenery, head back down the way you came. Be careful descending, because several sections of the trail are steep and badly eroded. The author wound up on her butt a couple of times coming down.

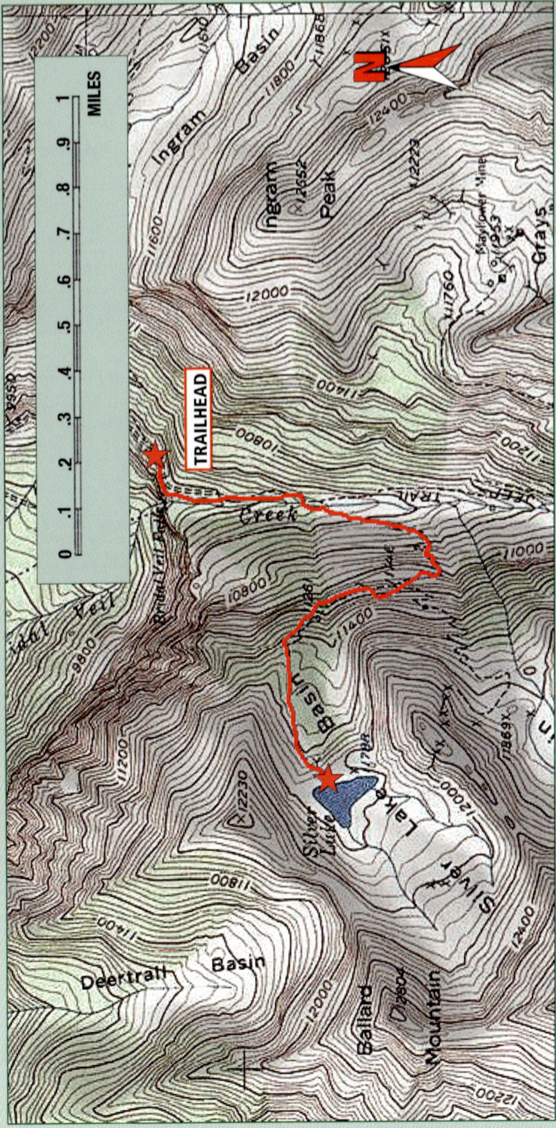
0 .1 .2 .3 .4 .5 .6 .7 .8 .9 1
MILES
TRAILHEAD
Ingram
Basin
Ingram
Peak
Creek
Basin
Silver
Lake
Lake
Silver
Deertrail
Basin
Ballard
Mountain
Grays

16. Uncompahgre Riverway Trail

BY ROD MARTINEZ

MAPS	Trails Illustrated, Telluride/ Silverton/Ouray/Lake City, Number 141; USGS, Ridgway 7.5 minute
ELEVATION GAIN	Minimal
RATING	Easy—Wheelchair-accessible
ROUND-TRIP DISTANCE	2.0 miles
ROUND-TRIP TIME	1 hour
NEAREST LANDMARK	Ridgway

COMMENT: Ridgway often is referred to as "The Gateway to the San Juans." As you travel from Telluride to Ridgway, you pass alongside the Sneffels Range, which is dominated by Mount Sneffels. Colorado 62 crosses over Dallas Divide, where you get spectacular mountain views in the fall and winter.

Ridgway is a terrific location to explore the stunning mountains and fertile valleys of southwestern Colorado. The town was founded in 1890 as headquarters of the renowned Rio Grande Southern narrow-gauge railroad and was the center of transportation for the area's rich silver and gold mines, ranches, and farms.

There are numerous recreational opportunities in and around the Ridgway area, such as four-wheeling in the high country on 100-year-old mining roads and taking photos of historic ghost towns and abandoned mines. You can also hike or bike on an extensive trail network, all the while surrounded by spectacular wildflowers, waterfalls, and wildlife.

Dennis Weaver Memorial Park in Ridgway is dedicated to the memory and vision of actor/environmentalist Dennis Weaver. This 60-acre public park is a permanent wildlife preserve along the lush Uncompahgre River corridor.

This bronze sculpture of a bald eagle in flight greets visitors at Dennis Weaver Memorial Park in Ridgway, one of two starting points for the Uncompahgre Riverway Trail. PHOTO BY ROD MARTINEZ

Within the park are miles of winding hiking and biking trails with spectacular mountain and river vistas. A highlight of the park is a 21-foot bronze eagle in flight. After your hike, you can drive the Western Movie Trail and walk locations featured in the original movie "True Grit."

GETTING THERE: From Telluride, head west on Colorado 145 (stay straight, rather than turning left toward Rico) for a little more than 15 miles. Turn right on Colorado 62 and drive 23 miles to the town of Ridgway. Measuring from the traffic light in Ridgway (intersection of U.S. 550 and Colorado 62), travel 1.5 miles north on U.S. 550, then turn left (west) at RiverSage Drive. Follow the road across the bridge and park in the lot on the right. You are now at Dennis Weaver Memorial Park.

Walking the Uncompahgre Riverway Trail takes you past a memorial to the Colorado Youth Corps. PHOTO BY ROD MARTINEZ

THE ROUTE: The Uncompahgre Riverway Trail can be hiked one of two directions. The trail can be accessed from the town of Ridgway at the Railroad Bridge or Memorial Park, and you will hike north. The hike, as described here, will start at Dennis Weaver Memorial Park and proceed south to the Railroad Bridge or Memorial Park.

The park is situated along the Uncompahgre River corridor. The trail begins a few yards north and west of the impressive eagle sculpture. The paved, wheelchair-accessible trail takes you along the river. Restrooms are available at the "Riverbend" section of the trail.

As you hike this easy but picturesque trail, keep your camera ready to photograph the abundant wildlife you might encounter. Early morning is the best time to see and photograph deer, marmots, golden eagles, mink, red fox, an assortment of waterfowl, and, at times, osprey and black bears. Bald eagles and elk are prevalent in the winter months.

This 2.0-mile round-trip hike can be taken any time of the year. During the winter, a fresh snow can make for a great snowshoe excursion. During late fall and winter, I have seen as many as six bald eagles. On a clear day, as you hike south toward Ridgway, the impressive Sneffels Range always is in view.

Just north of Dennis Weaver Memorial Park is Ridgway State Park, which offers many amenities depending on the time of year, including boating, camping, fishing, and numerous hiking trails. A state park fee is assessed for use of Ridgway State Park.

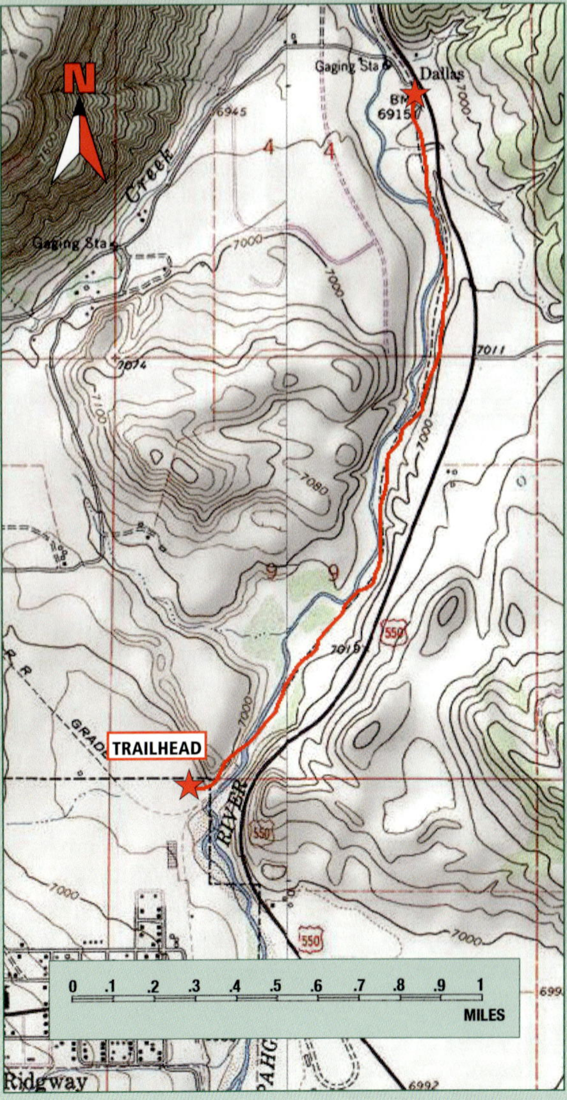
N
Gaging Sta
Dallas
BM
6915
7000
6945
Creek
Gaging Sta
7000
7000
7011
7074
7100
7000
7080
7019
550
R R
GRADE
TRAILHEAD
RIVER
550
7000
550
7000
0 .1 .2 .3 .4 .5 .6 .7 .8 .9 1
MILES
Ridgway
6992

17. Wetterhorn Basin Trail

BY SANDY HOAGLAND

MAPS	Trails Illustrated, Telluride/ Silverton/Ouray/Lake City, Number 141; USGS, Courthouse Mountain 7.5 minute; Latitude 40, Telluride/Silverton/Ouray
ELEVATION GAIN	1,750 feet from four-wheel-drive trailhead to pass; 2,450 feet from four-wheel-drive trailhead to basin (add 250 feet from two-wheel-drive trailhead)
RATING	Moderate
ROUND-TRIP DISTANCE	8.6 miles from four-wheel-drive trailhead; 2.8 miles more from two-wheel-drive trailhead
ROUND-TRIP TIME	4–5 hours to pass, 6–7 hours to basin
NEAREST LANDMARK	Ridgway

COMMENT: Considered a favorite day hike by many locals, this lovely hike in the Uncompahgre Wilderness passes through alpine meadows surrounded by stunning mountains and waterfalls. Wildflowers usually are plentiful in midsummer, and those with a keen eye might spot some wildlife. Snow may remain in the basin until early July, especially on the approach to 12,500-foot West Fork Pass. The West Fork of the Cimarron River and its tributaries also might be harder to cross before mid-July. Most of this hike is above treeline, so an early start during summer months is prudent to avoid afternoon thunderstorms. There are several primitive camp spots along Forest Road 860 for those who enjoy spending evenings under the stars.

GETTING THERE: From the traffic light at the intersection of U.S. 550 and Colorado 62 in Ridgway, it is 21.8 miles to the

Wetterhorn Peak (14,015 feet) rises dramatically over Wetterhorn Basin.
PHOTO BY SANDY HOAGLAND

four-wheel-drive trailhead, mostly on dirt roads. Following the signs to Owl Creek Pass covers the first 18 miles of the route. Start measuring mileage at the traffic light in Ridgway, and travel 1.8 miles north on U.S. 550 to a right turn (east) on County Road 10. At 2.7 miles, bear left toward Owl Creek Pass and Silver Jack Reservoir, staying on CR 10. At 4.5 miles, continue straight on County Road 10. At 6 miles, bear right on County Road 8. Go left at 7.5 miles, staying on CR 8. The Uncompahgre National Forest boundary is at mile 10, where the road becomes Forest Road 858. Bear left again at 11 miles. Continue on FR 858 to Owl Creek Pass at 18 miles. At 18.3 miles, take a right onto Forest Road 860. The first 2.1 miles of 860 is passable for passenger cars, and there is some room to park a few vehicles where the road starts to get rough. High-clearance four-wheel-drive vehicles can drive an additional 1.4 miles to the trailhead, crossing the West Fork of the Cimarron River 0.7 mile beyond the two-wheel-drive parking area. Some parking also is available at the river.

THE ROUTE: If starting from the two-wheel-drive parking area, hike 1.4 miles up the road to the four-wheel-drive trailhead. You will cross the river at 0.7 mile. There is no bridge at the river, so wading or rock-hopping is necessary.

Hikers ascend West Fork Pass en route to Wetterhorn Basin.

PHOTO BY SANDY HOAGLAND

The trail (#226) is well-defined all the way to West Fork Pass, 3.1 miles from the four-wheel-drive trailhead. The route begins in an alpine meadow but soon travels through a spruce forest, crossing several rocky drainages that drop dramatically from the ridge to the east. These drainages should be passable without much difficulty in summer months. Blazes on trees help mark the way if the trail is hidden beneath snow.

About 1.5 miles from the trailhead, the forest gives way to alpine meadows, revealing the many dramatic peaks surrounding the basin. The trail winds through boulder fields as it climbs toward the pass. The last 0.5 mile to West Fork Pass climbs more steeply, making secure footing difficult in a few spots. At the pass, views open up to the south, including the Cow Creek drainage and the mountains beyond it.

It is another 1.5 miles and 700 feet loss of elevation to Wetterhorn Basin, so be sure that storm clouds are not building before committing to this stretch. A short hike down the trail will reveal impressive views of the south side of Coxcomb Peak and 14,015-foot Wetterhorn Peak. The trail becomes less distinct on this side of the pass, with Cow Creek Trail and Coxcomb Trail intersecting before reaching the basin, so carefully follow the signs to stay on the correct trail.

After enjoying the beauty and serenity of Wetterhorn Basin, reverse the route to return to the trailhead.

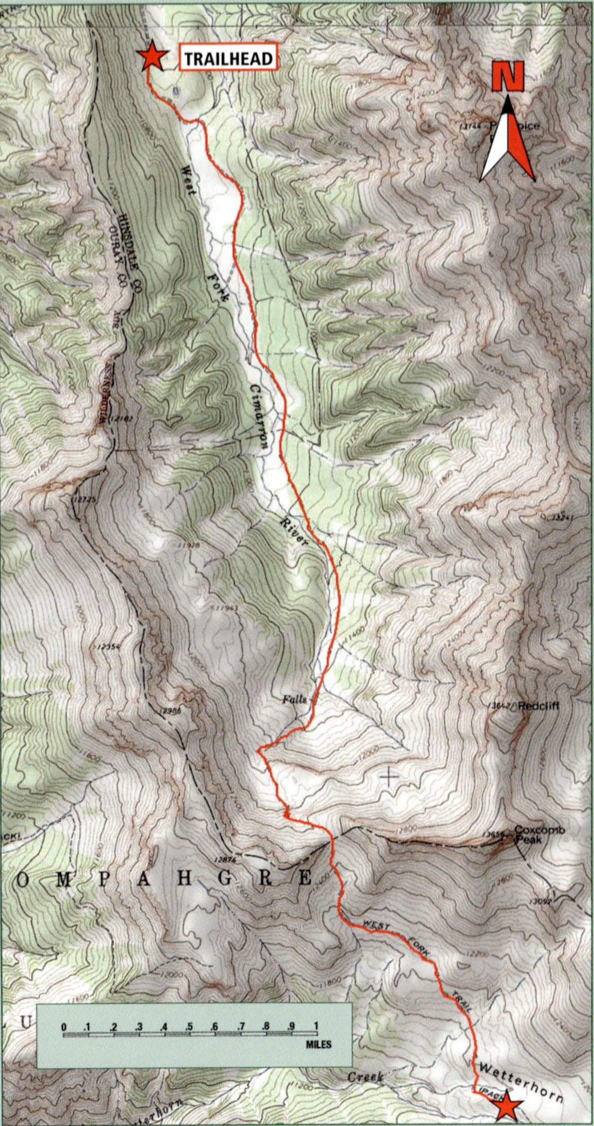
TRAILHEAD
N
West Fork Cimarron River
HINSDALE CO
OURAY CO
Falls
Redcliff
Coxcomb Peak
O M P A H G R E
WEST FORK TRAIL
Wetterhorn
Creek
0 .1 .2 .3 .4 .5 .6 .7 .8 .9 1
MILES

18. Wilson Meadows Trail

BY DIANA DONNELLY

MAPS	Trails Illustrated, Telluride/Silverton/Ouray/Lake City, Number 141; USGS, Mount Wilson 7.5 minute; Latitude 40, Telluride/Silverton/Ouray Trails
ELEVATION GAIN	980 feet
RATING	Easy to Moderate
ROUND-TRIP DISTANCE	6.0 miles
ROUND-TRIP TIME	4–5 hours
NEAREST LANDMARK	Lizard Head Pass

COMMENT: Wilson Meadows lies in all its glory at the base of some of the most remarkable landmarks in the San Miguel Mountains, which are surrounded by the Uncompahgre National Forest just southwest of Telluride. It is a good choice for those who would like to reach an area with breathtaking views from an easy trailhead access and for those who like a shorter-duration hike than most trails in the area.

The Lizard Head Trail and Wilson Meadows Trail host an abundance of wildflowers in summer and entice mushroom hunters in late summer. The area also is a popular archery-hunting destination in late summer and early fall. To reach Wilson Meadows, the more direct and quickest way is by way of the Lizard Head Trail from Lizard Head Pass.

GETTING THERE: From Telluride, take Colorado 145 south about 12.5 miles through magnificent mountain scenery to Lizard Head Pass. Turn right into the parking area, which has a grand view of the mountains to the east. You can park here and access the trail to the north or drive past the bathrooms to a short side road leading up a small hill to a substantial parking area at the main trailhead. The trail is

Lizard Head looks down on Wilson Meadows at the end of summer.

PHOTO BY DIANA DONNELLY

open to hikers and horseback riders and not open to bikers, ATVs, or any other motorized vehicles. Other wilderness guidelines apply.

THE ROUTE: Begin on the Lizard Head Trail (#505) at 10,240 feet. Meander through meadows with lush wildflowers until you enter a pleasant forest. The smell of fir is immediate as you pass over some babbling brooks until you arrive at a boulder/talus slope. You'll arrive at the Lizard Head Wilderness sign at approximately 1.5 miles.

Soon after, the trail starts to switchback and then continues to rise significantly up a talus slope with impressive views to the east of Trout Lake and its surrounding peaks. You will reach a patch of massive fir trees, then continue up and arrive at an avalanche scar area. There are many downed trees and large boulders that are home to marmots and pika. This is a good spot for a water break while viewing the peaks to the east, including high Thirteeners Pilot Knob, Golden Horn, and Vermilion Peak.

Back on the trail and heading northwest, you will pass a spruce/fir forest with clumps of Indian paintbrush. At 10,950 feet, you will see a sign where the Lizard Head Trail branches

The hike to Wilson Meadows begins in another meadow on the Lizard Head Trail at Lizard Head Pass. PHOTO BY DIANA DONNELLY

to the left to summit Black Face and continues to join the Cross Mountain Trail near Lizard Head. Veer right on the Wilson Meadows Trail (#512). The trail soon travels through a significant spruce/fir forest with many downed trees and much reindeer moss. Then the trail opens to a small meadow, where you are treated to a dramatic vista of the surrounding peaks. There is a Wilson Meadows Trail sign here.

As you continue, use caution while descending a black slope (decomposing Mancos shale), which can be slippery, especially when wet. Near the bottom of the shale slope a cairn marks a right-hand turn that takes you through alternating sections of meadow and forest. You will need to traverse another shale ridge (forested) and descend before arriving at several nice campsite areas. The trail then emerges from the forest to a panoramic view of Wilson Meadows in the foreground with Black Face to the south, Lizard Head to the west, Sunshine Peak to the northwest, and San Bernardo Mountain to the northeast. In the summer, a bountiful array of wildflowers fills the meadow and streams emerge from several directions to form Wilson Creek.

It's hard to leave the splendor of Wilson Meadows. When you do, just retrace your steps.

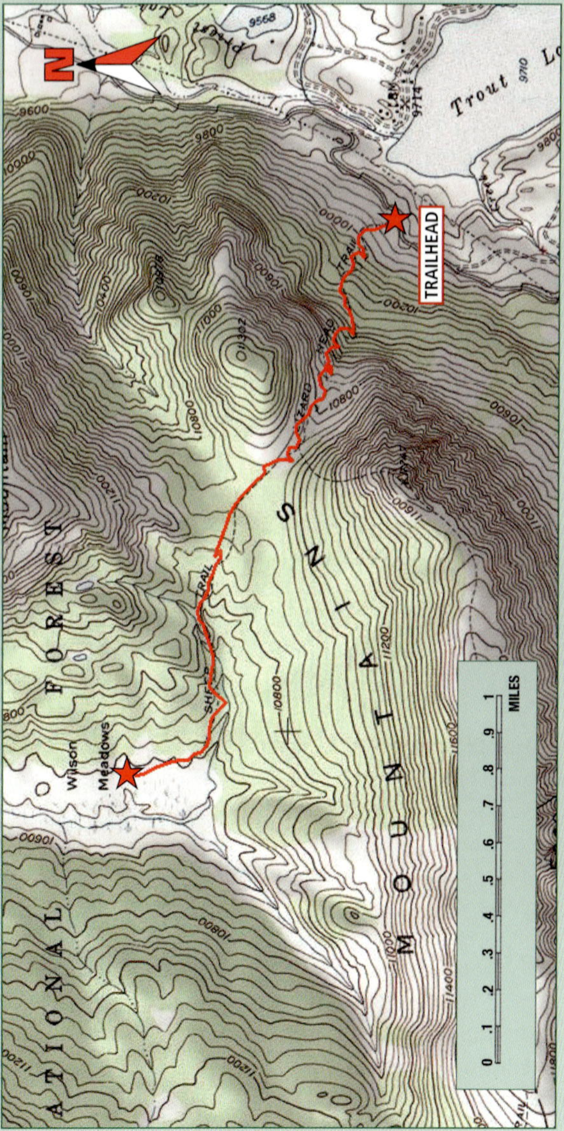
TRAILHEAD
Wilson Meadows
SHEEP HEAD TRAIL
MOUNTAINS
NATIONAL FOREST
0 .1 .2 .3 .4 .5 .6 .7 .8 .9 1
MILES

19. Wilson Mesa Trail

BY JEFF EISELE

MAPS	Trails Illustrated, Telluride/Silverton/Ouray/Lake City, Number 141; USGS, Gray Head 7.5 minute; Latitude 40, Telluride/Silverton/Ouray Trails
ELEVATION GAIN	1,600 feet
RATING	Moderate
ROUND-TRIP DISTANCE	7.8 miles
ROUND-TRIP TIME	4–6 hours
NEAREST LANDMARK	Telluride

COMMENT: The Wilson Mesa Trail extends for about 13.5 miles along the northern edge of the Lizard Head Wilderness, a few miles west of Telluride. There have been changes to the trail over the years, rendering some existing maps inaccurate. There are trailheads at either end, as well as two others in the middle, allowing for numerous round-trip and point-to-point possibilities.

The route described here is a middle section of the trail with great views of 14,017-foot Wilson Peak and Lizard Head, the 13,113-foot pinnacle for which the adjacent wilderness area is named. The accompanying map shows the described segment ending at Bilk Creek, as well as the east end of the trail to Sunshine Mesa, which adds 3.2 miles one-way.

This is a popular trail with a variety of users. Motorized trail bikes are allowed from July 1 through Labor Day, so if you're seeking a quieter experience, plan a visit in the fall when the abundant aspens are in their glory. Because the entire length of the trail lies below 10,500 feet, it generally is open and clear of snow earlier and later in the year.

Colorful aspens and dramatic Wilson Peak, a Fourteener, greet hikers on the Wilson Mesa Trail in autumn. PHOTO BY JEFF EISELE

GETTING THERE: From the "Society Turn" roundabout west of Telluride on Colorado 145, go west on 145 toward Placerville for 6 miles and turn south (left) on Silver Pick Road (County Road 60M). Go 4 miles and turn right onto County Road 59H (Forest Road 622). Proceed 2.3 miles to the trailhead parking area on your left at a junction with Forest Road 645, which branches off to the right. Park here.

Those who want to explore the western section of the Wilson Mesa Trail and others in the area can drive 2.3 miles up Forest Road 645 to the end of the road at the Rock of Ages Trailhead.

THE ROUTE: The first 2.8 miles of the trail is a series of alternating up and down sections between 9,800 and 10,000 feet elevation. In the last mile, you descend 520 feet as the trail swings south to Bilk Creek. Most of the climbing is on the return—in all, you gain 450 feet and lose 1,150 feet between the trailhead and Bilk Creek, crossing numerous small creeks along the way.

The hike starts in a mixed pine forest. As you proceed, though, you encounter progressively larger groves of aspens interspersed with meadows. It's breathtaking in autumn.

About 2.5 miles into the hike, you come to an open slope on the edge of a large aspen glade that provides the first open

Wilson Peak provides a stunning backdrop to "Lake Jake" along the Wilson Mesa Trail. PHOTO BY JEFF EISELE

view of Wilson Peak to the south and distant San Juan summits to the northeast. The scenery seems to get better around each turn over the remaining 1.4 miles to Bilk Creek.

After 2.9 miles, you pass through a gate and begin the final descent to Bilk Creek. At 3.3 miles you come to a small lake, identified as Lake Jake on the Latitude 40 map, that affords another stunning view of Wilson Peak. Farther south, Lizard Head also comes into view.

As you arrive at Bilk Creek, there's a sign that indicates it is 5 miles to the Silverpick Road where you started. It actually is 3.9 miles on the trail.

If you want to explore more but don't want to go all the way to the Sunshine Mesa Trailhead, the trail is relatively flat over the next 0.7 mile as it follows Bilk Creek to the intersection with the Lizard Head Trail. This is a mostly open area with expansive views to the north and south, and offers more impressive views of Lizard Head.

Retrace your steps back to the trailhead.

Lizard Head rises in the distance as you descend the Wilson Mesa Trail to Bilk Creek. PHOTO BY JEFF EISELE

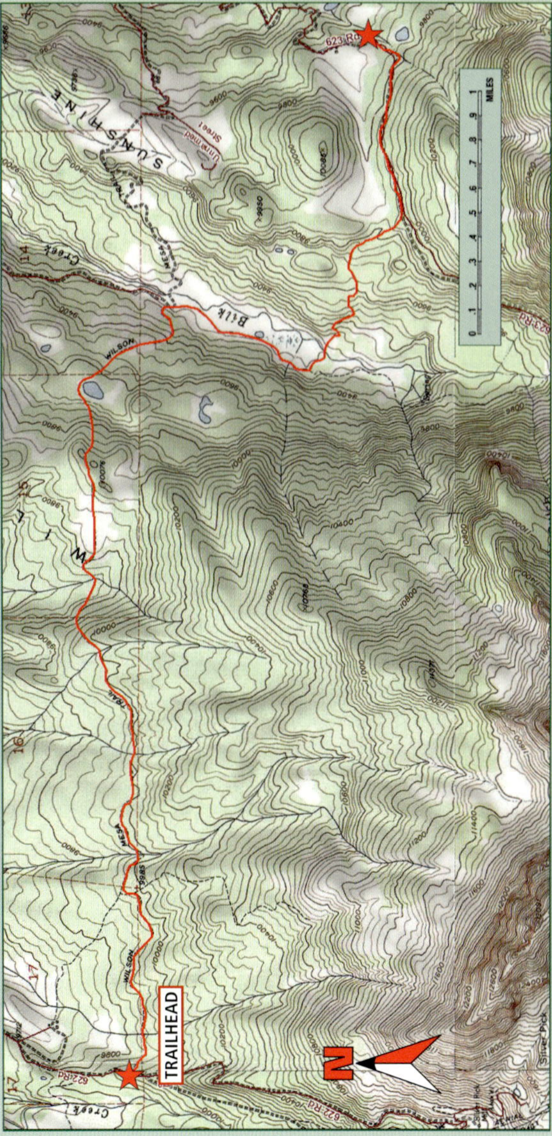
TRAILHEAD
623 Rd
622 Rd
WILSON
MESA
TRAIL
Bilk
Creek
SUNSHINE
Unnamed Street
MILES
Silver Pick
N

20. Woods Lake-Navajo Lake Trail

BY JEFF EISELE

MAPS	Trails Illustrated, Telluride/Silverton/Ouray/Lake City, Number 141; USGS, Little Cone and Dolores Peak 7.5 minute; Latitude 40, Telluride/Silverton/Ouray Trails
ELEVATION GAIN	2,330 feet
RATING	Difficult
ROUND-TRIP DISTANCE	8.8 miles
ROUND-TRIP TIME	5–7 hours
NEAREST LANDMARK	Woods Lake Campground

COMMENT: This hike takes you from Woods Lake on the western end of Wilson Mesa south into the Lizard Head Wilderness to a high basin surrounded by three of Colorado's Fourteeners. You hike through mixed aspen forest and top out just above treeline around 11,500 feet. The route traverses near this level for about a mile as you round the ridge on the north side of your destination, Navajo Basin, then descends and joins the Navajo Lake Trail for the last 0.5 mile to Navajo Lake. There are numerous campsites around the lake for those who want to extend their stay and explore the area. It is a popular departure point for climbers attempting to scale the peaks surrounding the basin, including Wilson Peak (14,017 feet), Mount Wilson (14,246), and El Diente (14,159), as well as Gladstone Peak (13,913), a Centennial (highest 100 in Colorado).

GETTING THERE: From the "Society Turn" roundabout west of Telluride on Colorado 145, go west on 145 toward Placerville for about 10 miles and turn south (left) on Fall Creek

Dolores Peak and Middle Peak are reflected in Woods Lake a short distance from the Woods Lake Trailhead. PHOTO BY JEFF EISELE

Road (Forest Road 618). Follow this road for 8.8 miles to the large trailhead parking area next to Woods Lake Campground. A large signboard with a map and information marks the trailhead on the east side of the road, east of the parking lot.

THE ROUTE: Follow the trail for 0.25 mile to a junction with connector trails for the Wilson Mesa Trail, which branches to the left (north), and the Lone Cone Trail, which branches to the right (west). You want to go straight: The sign indicates the Elk Creek Trail junction is 2.5 miles ahead.

You soon pass into the Lizard Head Wilderness and about 0.25 mile later cross an unnamed creek. The trail travels through mixed forest for about a mile, then turns east, continuing a steady climb. Along the way, you're treated to views to the west of the high ridgeline dominated by Dolores Peak (13,290) and Middle Peak (13,261).

The trail gets steeper as you reach treeline at 11,200 feet, and you soon reach an unmarked post at the junction with the Elk Creek Trail coming in from the left (northeast). This is 2.8 miles from the trailhead and a good turnaround point if you want a shorter hike and/or want to avoid the 500-foot climb out of Navajo Basin on the return. You also could

A view from the lower section of the Woods Lake Trail. PHOTO BY JEFF EISELE

venture partway down the Elk Creek Trail, which offers nice views to the north.

Go right (south) at the junction. In the next mile, the trail contours around the eastern end of a ridge of unnamed Thirteeners that forms the northern wall of Navajo Basin. After rounding this ridge, you will see the basin, as well as expansive views into the Dolores River Valley to the south. El Diente is prominent on the eastern end of the ridge on the south side of the basin, and farther east, the top of Mount Wilson is barely visible sticking up above lower slopes. Take a moment to admire them now—or do so on the return—because the farther you descend into the basin, the more they recede from view behind lower slopes. You'll have good views of Gladstone Peak at the head of the basin, as well as the unnamed Thirteeners to the north, all the way to the lake.

The last 0.75 mile is a 500-foot descent into the basin. The Navajo Lake Trail merges from the east about 0.5 mile before the trail reaches the lake. Remember that you'll have to ascend this section on the return to the trailhead.

Those planning to camp in the area should know that campfires are prohibited in Navajo Basin and within 100 feet of lakes in the Lizard Head Wilderness. Retrace your steps back to the trailhead at Woods Lake.

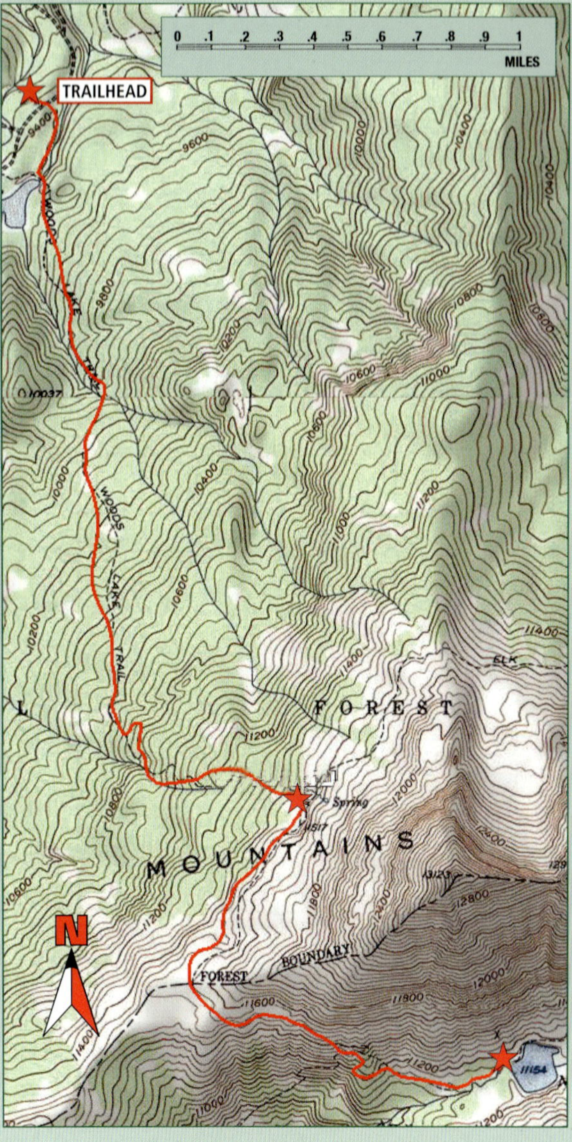
0 .1 .2 .3 .4 .5 .6 .7 .8 .9 1
MILES
TRAILHEAD
WOODS LAKE TRAIL
WOODS LAKE TRAIL
FOREST
MOUNTAINS
Spring
FOREST BOUNDARY
ELK
N
9400
9600
9800
10000
10200
10400
10600
10800
11000
11200
11400
11600
11800
12000
12400
12800
13123
11517
11154
10037

About the Author

Rod Martinez has always loved spending time outside. As a kid growing up in Cripple Creek, he explored the nearby hills and old mines. As he grew older, he found another love—photography. In time he discovered 35mm photography and a lifelong passion was born. Rod has climbed 17 of Colorado's 14ers and has hiked in almost all of the Western states, primarily in Colorado, Utah, and northern Arizona. He has been able to combine his two passions to visually capture nature's beauty on every hike. His work has resulted in Rod being named Grand Junction's Photographer of the Year for four years in a row. In 2001, he helped form the Southwest Photographic Arts Association Camera Club and currently teaches photography and leads photo workshops. Rod joined the Colorado Mountain Club in 2000 and has served as the program director for the Western Slope Group and currently acts as treasurer and trail steward for the group. He is the author of *The Best Grand Junction Hikes*, as well as a regular contributor to *Trail and Timberline.*

A view from the Woods Lake Trail of Dolores Peak on the return from Navajo Lake. PHOTO BY JEFF EISELE

Sunrise on Mount Sneffels. PHOTO BY ROD MARTINEZ

Checklist

THE BEST TELLURIDE HIKES